Early Praise For Bootstrapping 101

"Once again Bob Reiss captures the complexity of entrepreneurship with clarity and the 'wisdom of experience'. A must read for all those contemplating the 'Road Less Traveled,' creating opportunity for oneself."

—John W. Altman
Retired Professor of Entrepreneurship, Miami University, Babson College
Founder of six companies

"Those of us who have known Bob since Columbia College days respect his enormous command of entrepreneurism, taking ideas and hope to fruition and success. Bob uniquely covers all bases, keeps it simple and on target, and always focuses on the goal—taking entrepreneurial ideas successfully across the finish line. I highly recommend *Bootstrapping 101* to you."

—John A. Cervieri, Jr.
Founder Property Capital Trust,
which became an American Exchange Co.

"*Bootstrapping 101* is about as "nuts and bolts" as you can get. Hard hitting . . . easy to read . . . no fluff. Bob Reiss has given us a reference manual on how to get things done, quickly and with limited resources. Interwoven throughout the "how to" tips are nuggets of wisdom on business conduct that should be emblazoned on everyone's forehead. Keep this one handy . . . it should be the most dog-eared book in your business collection."

—Gary Naumann
Lecturer in Entrepreneurship
and Director, Spirit of Enterprise Center, Arizona State University
Co-founder Toy Boat, a collection of specialty toy stores

"Bob Reiss provides invaluable advice to anyone wanting to start his own business. In an open and easy-to-follow format, he presents tools and techniques that are not commonly thought of by the aspiring entrepreneur but can shave off months, if not years, of trial and error. A must read for anyone serious enough to venture in to the mine fields of starting a new business."

—**Herbert Beyenbach Score**
Counselor,
former VP, Citibank International

"Reiss has drawn on his experience as a successful entrepreneur to offer practical tips on how to succeed in business with minimal or no cash outlays. His writing style is down to earth, his tips are priceless."

—**Dr. lawrence Klatt**
Professor of Entrepreneurship

"Reiss not only has great ideas for Bootstrapping, but he has made them work. An insightful thinker, he analyzes what is effective and willingly shares it. The best guide to doing it yourself available."

—**William J. White**
Retired CEO/Chairman, Bell & Howell,
author and professor, Northwestern University

"Bob Reiss has done it again. In a simply written, easy-to-digest book Bob Reiss gives street-wise advice to aspiring entrepreneurs on how to stretch their dollars and spend creativity rather than cash. I'm a huge fan of the Reiss philosophy."

—**Murray B. Low, PhD**
Director, Eugene Lang Entrepreneurship Center,
Columbia Business School

"*Bootstrapping 101* is an essential part of any owner's (entrepreneur's) tool kit. It will inspire you to think in creative ways to reach your business objectives. Bob shares his concrete ideas to turn your business dreams into reality with real world experiences."

—**Amy Love**
founder Real Sports *magazine*

Bootstrapping 101

TIPS TO BUILD YOUR BUSINESS WITH
LIMITED CASH AND FREE OUTSIDE HELP

BOB REISS

R&R

6342 Via Venetia N
Delray Beach, FL 33484

The author gratefully acknowledges permission from Harvard
Business School Publishing for permission to use the Harvard Business
School Case R&R 386-019. Copyright © 1985 by the President and
Fellows of Harvard College.

This publication contains the opinions and ideas of its author
and is designed to provide useful advice in regard to the subject
matter covered. It is sold with the understanding that the author and
publisher are not engaged in rendering legal, accounting, investment,
or other professional services. Laws vary from state to state, federal
laws may apply, and if the reader requires expert assistance from a
registered investment adviser or legal advice, a competent
professional should be consulted.

The author and publisher specifically disclaim any responsibility
for any liability, loss, or risk, personal or otherwise, which is incurred as a
consequence, directly or indirectly, of the use and application of any
of the contents of this book.

Cover Design by Tim Kaage
Interior Design and Layout by Scribe Freelance

Library of Congress Control Number: 2009905825
ISBN: 978-0-578-02413-4

Printed in the United States of America

Acknowledgements

THIS IS THE SECOND BOOK that I've written. In the first one, *Low Risk High Reward*, I had a professional collaborator who proved immensely helpful. Since this book is about Bootstrapping, I decided to follow my own advice and write it alone (cost free) and get the free help of many others.

So, thank you to all the following for advice, editing, introducing, encouraging, and answering my endless array of questions.

John Altman	Len Green	Nancy Mathis
Herb Beyenbach	Howard Greene	Sumir Meghani
Amar Bhide	Michael Gustman	David Rains
Roy Birkett	Martha Hanlon	Stu Seltzer
Ian Calder	Howie Hansen	Sally Seston
Corinne Colbert	Mike Hsieh	Joe Sequino
Murray Eskenazi	Ohad Jehassi	Jereann Shafir
Donna Ettenson	Jaci Keeley	Howard Stevenson
Bert Goldberg	Rocco Loccisano	Peter Van
Morey Goldberg	Murray Low	Don Weiss
		Alan Zimmelman

Special thanks to the following for their above and beyond the call of duty in helping me get the book done:

Duane Barnes, John Cervieri, Larry Klatt, Amy Love, Gary Naumann, Jerry Shafir, Bill White, and Sherwin Zimring.

Most importantly, I want to thank my loving wife, Grace, for her indispensable aid in writing this book. She typed every word. Yes, I am the Neanderthal man who wrote every word by hand. She was instrumental in massaging my psyche and contributed in her understanding of the subject matter through her own Entrepreneurial experience. All this on top of being a great mother and wife.

Contents

CONTENTS

CONTENTS

Introduction

WHAT IS BOOTSTRAPPING? The dictionary definition is "to cause oneself to succeed without the help of others." The emphasis in most peoples' minds when thinking of Bootstrapping is without the help of others... do it on your own.

My thinking is very different. The emphasis should be on with the help of others. So, my definition is:

> *"To pursue success with limited resources*
> *and with the help of others."*

By limited resources, I primarily mean a shortage of money, a shortage of knowledge, and/or a shortage of helpful or essential contacts. These knowledge and contact shortfalls can emanate from lack of experience or know-how about the industry you're entering or business in general.

I assume you already have an idea and a passion for the venture and at least a rough plan... or you may already have an existing business.

This book is for existing small and medium business owners or managers and those about to start their own business. It is for people who find themselves with cash/knowledge shortages. Much of the subject matter is not taught in universities' business classes. Therefore, these Bootstrapping tips apply no matter your prior educational level. It is also for those with experience in the corporate arena. Starting a Small Business is a whole different world from the corporate one.

This book will offer you proven, practical, and workable tips to help you build your business. The emphasis is on tips that require little or no money and where and how to get free help, advice, consulting, or whatever you want to call it. Bootstrapping addresses solutions for your limited resources problem and points you to the vast array of free help available to you.

It will offer ideas on how to operate efficiently and how to get things done with no, or minimal, cash outlays as well as ideas on minimizing risk and staging risk. You will see that you do not need to raise as much money as you think or as you may be told. It will also help you preserve cash for the unexpected bumps in the road, like forgetting to plan for certain needed expenses.

The less money you need to raise, the more equity you can keep in your company, the sooner you can start the business, and the more money you will have to grow your existing business.

Finding ways to get things done with less or no money (Bootstrapping) is important because of the difficulty of obtaining money for start-ups and Small Businesses.

Banks are an inexpensive source of money but will not lend money to start-ups unless there are assets to back up the loans. That is their normal way of operating.

Venture capitalists are for very few companies. They may fund as few as three out of every 1,000 companies they look at. If you do not have experienced and knowledgeable leaders, your chances are almost nil. If you are successful, you will have to give up substantial equity.

Bootstrapping is a good discipline to instill in a company's culture. It will prevent wasteful spending when you have money. Steve Gordon, the founder of Restoration Hardware, said that if sufficient capital had been available to him in the company's early stages, he might not have been as successful as he was. The good habits formed by the early need for Bootstrapping will carry forward, even in good times, to prevent wasteful actions. In bad times Bootstrapping could mean survival.

One of the major attitudinal obstacles to success via Bootstrapping is ego control. You will have to do many things you never anticipate or think are beneath you. For instance, cleaning the floors and even your bathrooms. Many mundane chores like shopping for the cheapest supplies, ordering a phone, getting an email address, etc. are necessary. Your station in life might not play well at your school reunion. Or you could be the type of person who when lost won't stop to ask for directions. Somehow, in your mind, it's a weakness to seek help. Ego is interfering with good judgment.

Let me give you my personal example of ego. My first full time job was, in my opinion, a great one for learning, but to outsiders it might have looked like a loser. After four years in college, two years in the army, and a fresh MBA in my hand, I took a job with a pencil company. While most of my classmates were going to work for management consultants, IBM, General Electric, Procter & Gamble, etc., I interviewed with the president of Venus Pen and Pencil Company for the assistant to the president position. He quickly offered it to me.

It was a great sounding job to impress my peers. I quickly turned it down as it was a purely staff job. I wanted to do real work and take on responsibility. We continued to talk. He told me about a position that he felt I would not like. He wanted me to start a division that utilized the 100 pencil imprinting machines they owned and were stuck with. I would be on my own and would have to figure everything out myself. Every negative he put forth was a positive to me. In my mind, the man was telling me I could learn how to start a business on his buck.

My biggest problem was how do you tell your parents after all your years of schooling that your first big job is selling pencils?

The point is: all of these mental challenges are within your control. No cash is needed. You have the ability to deal with them.

In the 16 start-ups that I have been personally involved in, I've employed almost every one of the Bootstrapping tips that I offer in this book.

Here is a quick synopsis of one of those businesses. Trivial Pursuit began in Canada and was invented by two Canadians. I already had twenty years of experience in the toy-game industry and knew about Trivial Pursuit's great success in Canada. Shortly after its U.S. introduction, I decided that I wanted to develop my own Trivia game. At that time, my company, R&R, consisted of myself and a secretary. We were located in a small office in New York City.

Consulting with two of my New York Sales Reps, we decided the topic of our trivia game should be TV. Further, I decided that I needed a credible name to put on the game, and the logical one was TV Guide. At that time TV Guide had over an 18,000,000 weekly circulation, the second largest circulation in the country.

I then bought a TV Guide in my local supermarket to find their corporate address in Radnor, PA, and their publisher's name, Eric Larson. I wrote a short letter to Mr. Larson in mid October, asking for an appointment to present my proposal to develop a TV Guide Trivia Game. Shortly thereafter, I received a phone call from the Assistant Publisher, Bill Deitch. After two phone discussions and a follow up letter, I was invited to their home office to make my presentation. The result was we entered into a contract with no guarantees or up-front payments. I traded additional royalty points for 5 free full-page ads in TV Guide. (The cost to buy was $85,000 each.) Further, we contracted with them to create the 6,000 questions and answers we needed. This was a time sensitive project as we had to have a plan and a prototype ready for the February Toy Show and would need to begin shipments in May.

I started a new company called Trivia Inc. and brought in a partner for this venture who could provide the financing and administrative support required and whom I could trust. He was the owner of our advertising agency that we had worked with for over 20 years. This freed me to develop and market the game.

The end result was that we started shipping in May and voluntarily disbanded the company in December. A seven and a half month company life. We ended up selling 580,000 games at $12.50 each for a sales figure of $7,250,000 that produced a profit of $3,000,000. All with one full-time employee.

Harvard Business School wrote up this case to teach in their Entrepreneurial class. The R&R case continues after 20 years and is also taught in over 50 other graduate business schools.

For those of you who wish to study all the details of this case, it is shown in the appendix I, followed by my comments on each Bootstrapping tip that was used.

I bring this business example up to illustrate that these Bootstrap tips are not theoretical but real life actions. It is my hope and belief that many of the tips offered here will help you to make a success of your business.

1.
Barter

CONTRARY TO POPULAR BELIEF, Barter may be the oldest profession in the world. In prehistoric times, the tribe that controlled the hides traded with the tribe that controlled the fish. This probably continues today in many of the underdeveloped regions of the world.

In today's modern world, Barter has taken on different forms and has become a big business (estimated at $8-12 billion in the United States). It is essentially unchanged in that *Barter is the exchange of goods or services for other goods and services.* Usually, no cash is involved.

Barter today is being utilized by both large and small companies. Almost every imaginable product or service is bartered, including all types of media, clothing, toys, real estate, legal services, medical services, bakeries, hotels, restaurants, balloon rides, etc. The list goes on forever.

While most industries' business recedes in poor economic times, Bartering prospers with significant increases.

ADVANTAGES OF BARTER

- You receive goods or services your business needs without giving up any of your precious cash . . . an ultimate Bootstrapping weapon.
- If you are in a product business, you can dispose of excess or dead inventory at your full retail value. You need not take a markdown on your balance sheet. (This should please your banker, accountant, and shareholders if you are a public company.)

- Utilize your excess capacity if you manufacture a product or if you have excess time in a service business. There are many other businesses and people in the same boat as you. Both parties benefit and that is why Bartering is growing.

- Bartering can help you get new customers two ways. The person you Barter with is pleased with your product or service. When he wants more but has nothing to offer in trade, he will pay cash. Even better, that same pleased customer will recommend you to their friends and associates who will pay you cash when they buy. Word of mouth is still the most effective advertising tool there is. Barter exposes you to more mouths. However, do remember those mouths can also generate negative comments. Quality and reliability on your part will create the positive effect you want.

- If you have a seasonal business, Barter may be your answer in the slow cycles.

- You get full value for your product or service. There is no discounting. You also can control where your product is sold.

HOW BARTER WORKS

The most effective Barter works through exchanges. You sell your product to members of the exchange at full retail. In return, you get trade dollars which can be exchanged for other products' or services' value points with other participants of the exchange at any time.

In some exchanges, values over a certain amount are purchased through a blend of trade dollars and cash.

There are fees paid to the exchange for bringing the Barter protagonists together. Usually, the fees are about 12% and are borne equally between the two parties—6% each. In some exchanges, the full fee is borne by the buyer, and the seller pays nothing. Some exchanges charge a one-time fee to join, and some are free.

Dealing with expensive merchandise, the exchange may hold money for the goods until the buyer receives the product and is satisfied with the representations.

There are also many Barter transactions occurring without exchanges on a one-on-one basis.

Be aware that all Bartering transactions are taxable and must be reported to the IRS. You should consult with your accountant on this.

To locate the Barter exchange that best fits your needs, just go on the Internet and type in Business Bartering. There is also a trade association called IRTA (International Reciprocal Trade Association). Their address is:

524 Middle Street
Portsmouth, VA 23704
Phone: (757) 393-2292
Email: ron@irta.com
Website: **www.irta.com**

REAL LIFE BARTER STORIES

Lisa Medland founded New Management Solutions in 2002 and currently has seven employees. They are located in Coral Springs, Florida and specialize in Human Resource (HR) consulting and recruitment. She started her business in a shared office. As the company grew, they opted for their own offices. To furnish the offices and install a phone system, she tried Barter for the first time and saved her company over $15,000 in cash. The services she used to pay for her new office furnishings were HR audits, verifying employment files, creating employee handbooks, training, job descriptions, etc.

She was so pleased with her Barter experience that she has continued to Barter for as many things as she can, including travel, dining, etc. Lisa says that many of her Barter transactions have led to cash paying customers.

All her Barter is done through the Nubarter Exchange in Boca Raton, Florida, managed by Karen Roumay.

Going to the other end of the country, let's listen to Alan Zimmelman, the Director of Corporate Communications for ITEX, a large Barter Exchange, located in Bellevue, Washington with offices in 100 cities in the United States and Canada.

As Alan tells it, "A carpet cleaner went to a large home to complete a job; both the owner and the carpet cleaner were members of the same trade exchange. When the two-day job was completed, the homeowner asked the carpet cleaner (who did a sensational job) if he would like his pay in airline tickets? In the planning stages of his wedding, the carpet cleaner JUMPED at the chance to be able to fly to his honeymoon without laying out a ton of cash. The deal was made—clean carpets in exchange for two round-trip tickets to Europe."

The exchange put the two parties together, and the homeowner offered the carpet cleaner the tickets from his accumulated frequent flyer miles. A win-win with no cash exchanged.

Here is another exchange story as told by Alan: "A new restaurant was about to open in the Los Angeles, CA area, and the staff had just been hired and trained. The restaurant was approached by a Barter exchange to join. With a limited budget for advertising, the owner of the restaurant said 'sure.' Within days of opening the new establishment, trade exchange members were filling the empty tables. Most of the trade exchange members came with friends (who were not members). The food and ambiance were good—the friends returned (with more friends), and the restaurant was bustling with both trade and cash customers! The restaurant used their trade dollars to advertise in local newspapers and on the radio."

The trade exchange members who went to the restaurant paid with their exchange dollars. ITEX, through their local office, informed all their members about the restaurant's opening. Another win-win.

Alan told me a lot of charities get substantial contributions of trade dollars from people who want to support a charity but also want to conserve their cash.

He also told me that banks use Barter. He threw me with that one. I could see how the banks could use barter but could not comprehend what they could give in return to earn ITEX dollars. I would have bet my house they wouldn't give cash. Yes, I was right about that. What they offered was repossessed cars.

I think you can see Barter can be employed in every imaginable way. It's only limited by your imagination.

2.
Publicity

PUBLICITY IS THE GREAT wild card for small businesses. Certainly, advertising can be effective. However, a story in the media about you, your product, or your company generally carries far more weight and legitimacy than any paid for ads. Such a story is likely to reach both consumers and any intermediate customers, such as retailers. Because management generally has more time to read than buyers and other middle-level people, a news story or human-interest feature may have a disproportionate impact on decision makers. And finally, the cost to you can range from minimal (an investment of your time) to more substantial. However, it is usually lower than the cost of "equivalent" advertising.

How do you get started? If you have the money, hire a public relations firm. Try to retain a company that has prior experience with your kind of products or services and the kind of media you want to reach. If you are inclined to hire a large PR firm, ask to meet with the person who will be working directly on your account. In all cases, ask to see a proposed plan or approach to the job before you commit. I'd recommend interviewing more than one company, and I would definitely ask for and check references. This may surprise you, but I'd be suspicious of any PR people who "guarantee" results. Unlike advertising, there are no guarantees that something will appear in the media or that you'll *like* what appears.

You don't have to make a long-term commitment; you can hire a PR firm on a trial basis—say, ninety days. Once the firm is retained, plan on being an active participant in their activities. In general, reporters like to meet with the person who started the company or who is running it today. If that's you, be available and helpful. Make sure you understand and approve of the "angle" that your PR firm is pitching and to which media their angles are directed.

If you can't afford a PR firm, you can get the ball rolling yourself. One way is to go after your local newspaper. Think of that paper as a giant furnace that needs constant stoking and think of your story as tomorrow's (or next Sunday's) fuel. They may not know it, but they need you. Read the paper thoroughly and decide which department or columnist is the best fit with your product, service, or company. Make a phone call or write a letter to that department or individual, asking for an in-person meeting. This same approach can be employed with your local radio and TV stations.

In this initial overture and also in the follow-up meeting, your job is to pique their interest. Give them the kind of material they need. What's interesting about you? Is it the way you came up with the idea for the business? Is there something unusual in your background or the way the company is structured? Are you providing good jobs locally? Is your product indicative of a new trend?

Of course, this is harder to pull off if your local newspaper is the *New York Times* or the *Washington Post*. However, these media giants, too, need stories every day. Think creatively about the different sections of your targeted newspaper, especially if it's a major circulation daily, and determine which sections could possibly be interested in a story in addition to the business section?

Another valuable but generally more difficult approach is to pitch the wire services (Bloomberg, Reuters, Associated Press, etc.) directly. These companies are also in the "fuel-providing" business but on a large scale—a story from one of these services can appear in hundreds of newspapers, radio, and TV stations around the country. It is helpful to understand that the wire services and other media need you as much as you need them.

Remember, too, that this pipeline goes both ways. Stories by individual newspapers can get picked up by a wire service and garner national attention.

Don't overlook the other media that are out there either. For example, many consumer magazines for example run "new product" sections and "gift guides" for certain holidays (Valentine's, Mother's Day, Father's Day, Christmas, etc.). Someone in your company should regularly submit pictures and short descriptions of your new products to these kinds of outlets. You may be surprised at how many of these descriptions get picked up verbatim and how that translates into good orders. Similarly, most medium-sized and larger cities have at least one locally oriented magazine (*Boston, Philadelphia, New York, Miami,* and so on) that can be fertile ground for your story idea or new product description. Read the publication and write your ideas in the style the publication uses. The more work they have to do, the less your chances of inclusion. Note deadlines and publication lead times.

Industry magazines, newsletters, and newspapers are almost always excellent prospects for free publicity. In many cases they will run your releases about new products. Most have reporters on staff who are on the lookout for good stories for the next issues. Get to know them. There's a common misperception that you only get coverage in trade publications if you also buy advertising space, but in my experience that's not true. If you want to buy advertising, fine. It can't hurt your chances. But your immediate goal should be to sell them on your bright prospects. This is the news story they're looking for. And incidentally, the brighter your prospects look, the more likely it is that these media will look at you as a potential advertiser.

In many ways, TV is the most powerful medium of all. It's visual, visceral, and far better at evoking and implying things. However, the economic stakes are much higher, which makes it much harder to get attention from TV programs. So send those story ideas and new product descriptions to your local TV stations and follow up—but don't do so at the expense of other, more accessible media, including radio.

Amy Love, an entrepreneur, was very effective in promoting her start-up by soliciting local TV stations to appear as a guest to discuss her venture. Her success was predicated on her willingness to do what most people would not . . . namely get up at 4-5 a.m. to go to the TV studio.

Press Releases

The best way to initially approach the media is by sending one-page press releases to targeted media people. The release can be about you, your company, your product, your philosophy, the company's or your accomplishment, or any interesting fact of the above. Including relevant humor is a plus. This release via email or snail mail is the least expensive initial approach. If you use email, work hard to make the subject line compelling. Never include attachments unless a reporter specifically requests it. Cut and paste the press release in the body of the email.

If your target list is extensive, I would try sending a small amount initially (25). See how that works. If it doesn't alter your message, you could initially test different approaches to determine the most effective. I would simultaneously test email and regular mail. Email, of course, is less expensive, especially if your list is a large one.

After your initial foray, the key to the game is follow up. Your goal is to get a personal meeting or a phone interview.

When you are successful in getting your story printed or broadcast, promote it. Send it to your sales force, employees, investors, buyers, other stakeholders, and other media. The other media can be in different cities, different media, or national media. Your first story will give you credibility with other media.

Most of the time, I would not send unsolicited samples to the media. It is wasteful and more important will not be seen by your target. Also, in some peoples' minds, it cheapens your product. I would do everything to encourage the media person you are contacting to ask for a free sample.

Events and Promotions

Events and promotions are part of public relations. Done well, a promotional event can be an affordable and highly effective way of generating major sales of your product. I believe that money well spent in this arena gives you much more bang for your buck than traditional advertising. And because events call for more creativity than money, they are doubly suited for new and growing companies.

The best events and promotions are those that are designed specifically for your product or service. The tie-ins between the event and your product's benefits should be clear and memorable—not only to help sell the product but also to discourage competitors from trying similar stunts. If possible, hook up with an appropriate partner who can bring a major contribution to the table. (This could be money, a brand name, or marketing savvy.) If you use third-party individuals or organizations to help stage the event, you should make sure that everyone gets sufficient benefit from the event to give it their all.

Let me give an example from my own experience. Our company, Reiss Games, developed and introduced a line of magic. We designed full-color packaging to contain a collection of tried-and-true magic tricks that could be learned in a very short time. Fifteen minutes was our targeted learning curve. We purposely stayed away from tricks that required sleight-of-hand dexterity and also from tricks that professional magicians use to make their living.

To develop the line, I signed up for an evening course on magic that was taught by the celebrated magician, George Schindler. The course was geared to beginners like me, and it was a great deal of fun. Eventually, we signed Schindler to help us develop the line, and for a period of about two months, our office was a fun factory. George would come and demonstrate tricks that met our easy-to-learn requirement. We'd select a trick, cost out and fabricate its components, and develop a suitable line of patter that our customers could use. (Patter is a magician's word to connote what you say as you perform a trick. It helps to fool your audience, and we referred to it as "slight of mouth.") All told, we prepared a line of twenty-four kits and introduced them to the marketplace.

One of our customers was J.C. Penney, which sold our line through their catalog and retail stores. It was very successful for us and for them. As a result, we sat down with Penney to figure out a strategy for increasing sales of the magic kits.

Penney's buyer for the magic line was very bright and ambitious. He came up with the idea that we demonstrate the magic in his retail stores which he projected would drive up sales dramatically. We suspected he was right, but demonstrations are personnel-intensive and, therefore, very expensive. We declined this opportunity to become poor.

However, the Penney buyer loved our line, thought it had great upside potential, and kept after us. We knew we had to do something to satisfy this important customer, yet we couldn't figure out what we could do that would be both effective and affordable. Then I remembered one of the many conversations I had had with George Schindler.

Over lunch one day, Schindler had told me about the Society of American Magicians. This group had some 10,000 members at that time—mostly amateurs who had to demonstrate a certain skill level to gain acceptance into the society. Schindler had explained that one of the society's missions was to perpetuate the art of magic. One way they did this was to declare a "National Magic Week" every October. The goal of National Magic Week was to commemorate the death of escape artist, Harry Houdini, and to perpetuate the art of magic. During National Magic Week, magicians around the country performed in hospitals, nursing homes, and a variety of other venues where they could get an audience.

I remembered this conversation well. I also thought about the magicians I knew, including Schindler. They came from all different walks of life, but almost without exception, they loved magic. They loved performing a good trick well. They craved the spotlight and, in many cases, didn't get enough of it.

After thinking through the rough details of a plan, I asked Schindler to set up a meeting between the president of the Society of American Magicians and me. At that meeting I said that we could help the society in its goal of promoting magic and that we could put large numbers of magicians in front of appreciative crowds—in J.C. Penney stores. We couldn't pay these performers, but we could probably persuade Penney to run local ads featuring the event and the magician, including a promotional picture of the performer. The president was intrigued and suggested that I broach the idea at the society's upcoming national convention.

I immediately accepted this invitation. I then called a quick meeting with my Penney buyer and laid out my scheme. "I'm pretty sure I can get top magicians to perform in your stores at no charge," I told him, "if you can advertise the events and put the performer's name and picture in each ad." He said he was interested but would have to go up the ladder to find the necessary ad dollars. Together we went down the hall to Penney's head of Public Relations who controlled a healthy discretionary budget. The PR head liked the idea—so much so that he suggested that he accompany me to the society's convention. I assume that the fact that this meant three days in Miami Beach during the winter had some bearing on his decision.

The day came, and I proposed my deal to the assembled magicians. I emphasized that there would be no pay involved—only good publicity and most likely a good crowd. I ended my pitch by saying that when the meeting was over, Penney's PR director and I would be at a desk in the lobby, ready to sign up anybody who wanted to participate. We had no idea what kind of response we'd get. To our amazement, by the time we got to the lobby, we had scores of magicians standing in line, eager for the chance to sign up and perform.

Penney delivered on its part of the bargain magnificently. They produced an ad with a banner headline reading: "J.C. Penny and the Society of American Magicians Celebrate National Magic Week." Below the headline, the ad included the date and time of the demonstrations and a picture of the local performing magician. For our part, we hired (on a contract basis) a PR specialist who worked out of her house in California to coordinate the effort.

In my view, this was a win-win-win: Penney got their demonstrations at no cost to them, sold tons of merchandise, and earned excellent publicity and goodwill through their affiliation with the magicians. The society got far more publicity than it had ever received.

Individual magicians got their names and pictures in their hometown newspaper with the Penney "seal of approval" implicitly associated with them. We sold goods and greatly enhanced our relationship with a key customer—at hardly any cost to us.

The lessons I took away from this and similar experiences include the following:

- **Everything is possible.**
- **Understand people's emotional buttons** (e.g., many magicians crave recognition more than money).
- **Don't be embarrassed to state your intentions clearly and bluntly.** In this case we needed to get magicians to perform for us for no pay. Our frankness seemed to be appreciated.
- **Persistence can pay off in both directions.** In this case, the persistence of the Penney buyer set the stage for a very successful promotion. In other cases, it's been my persistence that made the difference.
- **Think outside the box.** Yes, this is becoming a tiresome cliché, but it captures the essence of a great promotion: how can we do something so fresh and different that the customer and consumer will find us irresistible?

The Internet can be the most impactful tool for your low cost Public Relations effort. In our next chapter on the Internet, we will offer tips and more food for thought.

3.
Internet Revolution

THE INTERNET HAS PROFOUNDLY and rapidly changed the way we communicate and do business in the United States and globally. It has had an impact on our lives comparable to the Industrial Revolution. Though still in its infancy, by mid March 2010, according to Internet World Statistics, 1.956 billion people worldwide were using the Internet with North America at 77.4% having the highest user penetration relative to population. As of April 2009, there were 231 million websites, a 46 million increase from the beginning of the year, according to Netcraft.

To give you some idea of the size of the Internet, here are some recent figures on individual companies. Remember, these companies are relatively young.

- Google revenue in 2010 was $29.3 billion, with most coming from "ad words," their advertising vehicle. They currently have a market cap of over $192 Billion and the most traffic in the world.
- Facebook started in 2004, was valued as a private company in 2010 at 50 billion dollars with Goldman Sachs raising $1.5 billion for them in a private offering.
- Groupon, at the end of its second year in business, was offered six billion to sell to Google, which they turned down.
- Amazon.com, known for its book selling, had revenues of over $19 billion dollars in 2008 and has a current market cap of over $32 Billion. It also is the prime reason for the precipitous decline of the retail book stores.
- Further, the Internet is a global phenomenon. Besides, its use in commerce and information, it has a major impact on

governments throughout the world. Transparency is the order of the day. Secrets are very difficult to keep and once one is revealed, it can go viral and reach every corner of the world immediately. Many dictatorial governments try to block out sites or shut down the Internet. It, however, is almost impossible to fully implement. Recent uprisings leading to a change of government in Tunisia and Egypt are examples of the power of the internet.

Although these are examples of large companies, do not assume that the Internet is only for big businesses. To the contrary, it's the best venue for small businesses to better compete with the "big boys." This is best illustrated in advertising. Anyone can buy local ads on the Internet. You can specify the zip codes you wish and for the budget you can afford.

Google's Ad Words and other sites will accept your ad and only charge you for the visitors that click on your site (called "pay per click.") You can start with a $200 budget. This is affordable, a Variable Cost, and a great way to test. Google claims that most of its clients and revenue emanate from small business.

The computer screen is the same size for a Fortune 500 company as Joe's corner grocery store. The Internet is a very democratic media. Anyone, regardless of income, background, race, gender, credit rating, etc., can have a web page on the Internet. Some are free. Of course, those companies with more money can afford to create better designed sites to more effectively generate web traffic through their spending.

There are two types of businesses using the web.

1. Those whose primary income is from the Internet.
2. Those that use the Internet to support their non-web business.

Almost all human and business activity is conducted on the Internet. In the business sector, products and services as diverse as education, cars, consulting, research, real estate, publicity, housewares, lawn services, flowers, gifts, gadgets, communicating, politics, apparel, pets, collectibles, books, used articles, charity giving, polls, news, information, and sports are offered, along with many, many more.

On the personal side, there is dating, keeping in touch with friends, voting, travel, investing, job searches, entertainment, game playing, and much, much more.

So whatever your business, you should be able to find some way to use the Internet to advance your business no matter the initial size of your budget. Your knowledge and smarts will serve you as well as cash.

The Internet, its strategies, nuances, costs, potential, etc. would apply to most chapters in this book. In nine of these chapters specific reference is made, usually to a website address to help you. In the Government chapter, there are references in all 10 of the agencies mentioned. Instead of weaving the Internet into each of these chapters, I felt it better to do so in this separate Internet chapter.

I see four main areas to explore.

1. **Creating a Website.**
   The cost to do so relates to your resources and strategic purpose.

2. **How Will People Find You?**
   The adage of having the best mousetrap doesn't mean you will have the most sales. Your potential customers need to know about your product or service.

3. **Getting Actionable Results From Those That Visit Your Site.**
   You need to achieve your web objectives and there are many strategies to do so.

4. **Monitor and Analyze All Your Website Activity.**
   As in all businesses, you should be prepared to change tactics and strategies based on what is happening. To do so, you first need to know what is going on.

The quantity of information available to everyone on creating a website is overwhelming. I just went to the two largest search engines and typed in "creating a website." Here's what came up.

On Google, there were over 400 million entries. Yahoo had over 1 billion. These numbers constantly fluctuate, but they are always of a high magnitude. At the same time, I went to Amazon.com to see how many books there were on creating a website. They listed 2,818. They offer new books, used books, e-books, and many are also available for Kindle readers. A large number of these are geared for beginners. Titles like *Building a Website for Dummies* and *Create Your First Website by 3:45 This Afternoon* are indicative of the genre.

The cost to learn about creating a website and how to use it are virtually nil. The websites you'll be directed to from Google and Yahoo are mostly free and book costs are minor. With all this information available to you, I don't see any purpose in trying to offer a tutorial about creating and marketing a website. I do believe, however, that it is very important to create a web presence for your company no matter its size or business type and to keep learning on how better to use it to advance your business.

Before you delve into creating a website and how to employ it, you should address and answer some key questions, such as:

- *What is the purpose of your website?*
  Your website objective will determine how and who builds it. If you are going to sell product, then special features must be installed to handle the payments for goods and the acknowledgement of orders and shipping of same. If your website is primarily to showcase your work like an artist or journalist, the website can be simple and less costly. Whoever builds it should know ahead of time your objectives, the demographics of your customer, what you are offering, and the benefits you are offering them.

- *Create your website or hire a pro.*

  A lot of the considerations in resolving this issue are your resources, your purpose, your knowledge, the people who can help you, etc. You will see a plethora of websites that will show you how to set up your site for free. As everything in life, the quality of people offering Free web services and For Fee services differ dramatically. There are many scams out there. You need to do your homework to screen the players. I would first look to people you know or their associates who have gone through the process of creating their websites. They should be able to offer you helpful insights. I would consider using some of the services or people mentioned elsewhere in this book for help and guidance, like SCORE, SBDC, Mentors, universities, etc. Students studying computer science can be a great no cost or almost free source for you. You might think about hiring a computer savvy student as an intern and give him/her real responsibility to enhance your website effectiveness. If they add value, I would consider paying them a cash bonus.

  You can also do this in stages. Early stage, where you are really cash poor, do your website yourself; as your company progresses, hire a web specialist to further improve your site.

- *Pre-Website Preparation.*

  Before creating a website, you should come up with a domain name, a host to run your site, and determine how you will track and analyze your web's activity.

  o **Domain Name**

  After deciding on the name you want, you need to ascertain if it is already being used by someone else. This is easy to do. I recently did this for this book, and you should realize that I fall into the computer challenged category. Fortunately, someone I know recommended going to the website <u>**www.GoDaddy.com**</u>.

First, I went to the spot to check out if anyone had the name I wanted. I then typed in "Bootstrapping101." (Didn't need to hire a consultant for that.) Word came back immediately that the name was clear. Cost—zero.

Then I quickly applied for the name on the same site. Filled out the credit card information with the name application and immediately received confirmation that I had my website. Cost--$10.19.

There are many other websites that offer this same service.

o   **Choose a Web Host**
Every web site must have a host.
www.4creatingawebsite.com, based on Google and Yahoo rankings, is one of the most popular sites for creating a website. www.4creatingawebsite.com says "A Web Host stores the website you create on their servers and transmits it to the Internet so that when someone types in your domain name, your website appears. A server is just a fancy computer that 'serves up' your website to the Internet."

This same site goes on to explain in detail how to choose a good web host and recommends hosts. There are many other sites that do the same. The bottom line is that you must have a host. The cost for a host currently varies from $4.95 to $29.95 a month with savings if you commit for a year.

o   **Analyzing the Visitors to Your Site**
The reason you want to look at this question upfront is that you can initially incorporate this analysis feature into your website. You can determine who comes to your site, what they look at there, how long they stay, what action they take, and more. Your Host can provide some of these answers as part of its fee, but the

consensus opinion is that "Google Analytics" is the best source for this information. Cost is zero.

Getting the right visitors to your website is a more formidable task than just creating a website. There are a vast array of strategies and nuances available. You will be dealing with Blogs, Search Engines, Key Words, Social Networks, Banner Ads, Pay Per Click, Megatabs, Search Engine Optimization, Email marketing, Article marketing, and more. Your decisions will be based on your resources, knowledge, and commitment to making the Internet work for you. As in creating a website, many of your actions are free and many for a fee. Your early actions will be somewhat dictated by what you can afford. As you grow your business and more cash is available, you can afford to invest more in your web.

Much of your web growth like business growth is based on your creativity, innovation, and **continuous learning**. Here is an example of a small company that creatively utilized its website to further their company's growth at little cost.

Winning Moves is a Toy/Game company located in Danvers Massachusetts, a suburb of Boston, that started in 1995. They created their first website: www.winning-moves.com the same year for e-mails and just to have a presence. According to their VP of Marketing, Joe Sequino, they revised the website in 2004 to sell their games through their website. The cost was minimal.

Winning Moves sold games nationally through toy and specialty stores. However, there were many parts of the country that did not have a local store carrying their games. They felt their website could address that problem.

The sale of games from their website did very well even though they refrained from discounting, a proven ecommerce strategy to maximize sales. They did so to protect their retailer customers by not undercutting them.

In 2006, they did a major upgrading of their site to accommodate their sales success, maintain and improve customer service, and make it easier to update the site. This revision was done by a professional company. However, at this point Winning Moves was a successful enterprise with the resources to fund this web upgrade.

They then started to use the Internet creatively to advance their position with their retailers, consumers, and Sales Reps. In addition, they started to film two-minute to eight-minute videos, explaining the merits of all their games. They then put over 25 videos on YouTube for the world to see. There was no cost to do this as Joe Sequino himself did the narration of each game on his home camera. This example of no cost utilization of a social Internet site has proven very successful.

Next, Winning Moves' sales manager will make short videos on best practice ways to sell the company's products that will be shown on YouTube. They can restrict the YouTube viewership just to people they want to invite to see these videos. This YouTube privacy feature is offered at no cost.

There are so many websites that are extremely helpful to your business and your life. And most of them are free. It seems that a new one pops up every day. I wanted to share these sites with you in an appendix. However, the changes are so rapid that it could be outdated quickly. So…I have created a list of these sites and put it on my website where we can continuously update them. To see them, just go to www.bootstrapping101.com/websites.

Whether you are a product or service company, an Internet only company, or a non-web business, a home based business or not, if you focus on the innovative ways to exploit the power of the Internet, you should be rewarded. You also should be able to compete on a more favorable basis with big companies. Small companies are generally more flexible, can act more quickly, and are not burdened by the politics inherent in most large companies.

Be aware that Internet strategies, companies and sources of information can get obsolete in a hurry. The Internet is a constant learning experience which best comes from personally exploring, trying, using, and adjusting to and with it.

4.
Free Advertising

PER INQUIRY ADS

ASSUME THAT YOU HAVE no advertising budget. How do you get the word on your product out there to your potential consumers at no cost to you?

One answer is per inquiry (P.I.) ads. How does this work? In most cases, media outlets (newspapers, magazines, radio, TV, etc.) fail to sell all of their advertising space. Think of ad space as the equivalent of hotel rooms. If a hotel room sits empty, its potential revenue is gone forever. The same holds true for ad space. When that show's broadcast ends or that newspaper or magazine hits the streets, the opportunity to sell space is over for that specific show or edition.

How do you take advantage of this? Easy. You prepare an ad with a coupon for direct response and give it to (for example) a magazine. They run the ad at no advertising cost to you. In return, you give them a percentage of the sale. This is a P.I. deal, and in my experience, it's a true win-win. The magazine gets a chance to generate some income where they otherwise would have generated nothing. The supplier generates some immediate sales and also gets a "free" ad that can help create name recognition.

Be aware that the P.I. approach requires you, as the supplier, to have the capability of shipping individual customer orders. The magazine's only involvement is to run the ad. After that, all inventory and fulfillment responsibilities belong to you.

I used a magazine for my example because that's by far the most common medium for P.I. ads although newspapers, TV, and radio outlets also accept them. In the case of electronic media, you will need to supply the completed ad in whatever format that station or network requests. Again, fulfillment is entirely your responsibility.

Many people think that P.I. ads are only run in third tier media. That is not true. We have run P.I. ads in major magazines like *Time, Golf, Field & Stream,* and *Modern Bride.* Some of our customers have run 1-800 TV response ads on our products, using the same TV stations from which they purchase commercials.

One word of advice: in many cases, you're better off not including your company name in the coupon. Some retailers with whom you're already working may feel—if they see your name in that coupon—that you're competing with them by drawing off some of their potential sales. I know that this kind of ad exposure can only help them, but it's not always an argument that they buy. In this case, be careful about a high company profile.

P.I. ads should be easier to obtain in poor economic times. One of the first budget cuts of corporations in a downturn is advertising. The media may not be able to sell all their advertising and thus will be more susceptible to P.I. ads.

Although it is not free, *pay per click* advertising (explained in the Internet chapter) is extremely inexpensive and an excellent tool for a small business.

5.
Selling

WHAT IS THE ONE THING you absolutely need to have for a business to succeed?
Answer: **CUSTOMER**

What do customers give you that sustains your company?
Answer: **ORDERS**

Now we have **CUSTOMERS** $\Rightarrow$ **ORDERS**
You might have thought the answer to the first question was orders, and it would be a good answer. However, *customer* is a better answer as only customers can give you reorders, the key to business sustainability. Orders don't create reorders.

Now what is the process of getting customers to give you orders?
Answer: **SELLING**

SELLING $\Rightarrow$ **CUSTOMERS** $\Rightarrow$ **ORDERS**

To complete the anatomy of a business, add a fourth element. The orders eventually turn into money or cash . . . your company's blood plasma. So, now you have the big four.

SELLING $\Rightarrow$ **CUSTOMERS** $\Rightarrow$ **ORDERS** $\Rightarrow$ **CASH**

Always remember the above. You will have many distractions, fires to put out, and competitive challenges. As you deal with all these important issues, never lose focus on the above big four. The customer is the key to your survival and growth. Only a *satisfied* customer will write a reorder. Every job function and employee in some way is involved in one or more of the above Big Four.

The reason the above is mentioned here is to put the sales function in perspective and show you how crucial it is to your company's success.

My definition of sales is "Persuading someone to take an action favorable to *all* parties." I emphasize **all** because many people are satisfied to receive an order for a product or service that is not of value to the customer. That's not a good thing as you will not get a reorder.

I know that many of you shudder at the thought of selling. You think that you were not born to be a salesperson. You don't have the charisma you think is required, the gift of gab, wining and dining customers is not your thing, you won't act unethically to get a customer, you're an introvert not an extrovert, you don't want to spend your life on the road, etc. Clear your head from all these mis-conceptions. There are no salesperson genes. SELLING IS AN ACQUIRED SKILL.

Hopefully you are now sold on selling's importance to your future. WHO SHOULD SELL?

Everyone, from the receptionist, the bookkeeper, the shipping clerk, etc., should be selling the virtues of your company and product to all the people with whom they come in contact. The most important salesperson is you, the Entrepreneur/President, particularly in the early stages of the company. He/she sets the tone and priority of the sales function and of satisfying customers. The selling effort by the head of the company costs the company nothing. No cash is expended, which is the ultimate bootstrapping effort.

As the company grows, the CEO will have less and less time for selling as his efforts will be transferred to hiring, managing, and motivating new employees, raising expansion money, pushing innovation, and exhibiting leadership. That is why you want to encourage and train all your people to act as salespeople.

Let's start at the front desk. The receptionist who answers the phone and deals with customers and potential customers is a key sales agent.

In my experience, many customers' overwhelming impression of a company is formed through their initial phone contact, which usually goes through the receptionists. We should give these people the title of "Director of First Impressions." So take care in their hiring, training, pay, and treatment.

HOW DO YOU LEARN TO SELL EFFECTIVELY?

Selling- is not taught in most business schools. There are many, many books and videos on the subject. I just checked "sales" on Amazon.com, and it showed 671,125 results. Overwhelming! There are some excellent books, but I have found that a great many are primarily inspirational. Your passion for your company should provide you with ample inspiration.

I believe selling can best be learned by doing it. The more you do it, the better you get. This is very similar to public speaking. You need to understand that sales rejection is not personal and should be expected. Every rejection is an opportunity to learn. To use a baseball analogy, a hitter who averages only one hit in every three attempts can go to the Hall of Fame. We strived to obtain an order in at least half of all the sales calls we made.

However, that being said, I will provide some insights and tips to help the sales learning process. Keep in mind you should develop your own style and not use someone else's prepared sales pitch.

WAYS TO SELL

I see five general ways to sell:

COMPANY SALES FORCE
SALES REPS
DIRECT RESPONSE
TRADE SHOWS
WALK-INS

The COMPANY SALES FORCE in the early stages is primarily the Entrepreneur/CEO for a number of reasons. There is not enough money to hire experienced, quality sales people. Potential customers are impressed that the boss is calling on them. The passion that the founder/president has for the company should come through, and it is a potent sales asset. Buyers tend to want to give passionate people a chance.

SALES REPS in the company's early stages are an ideal choice because they are completely a variable expense and cash is in short supply. Reps also provide value as they have established relationships with your prospective customers and have immediate access. I would suggest that early on, you make some sales calls with your reps. It gives you a reading on how effective they are; it gives you a chance to educate them on your product and company. You can hear a buyer's reactions to your offerings without the Sales Reps' filtering process. You get the chance to develop strategies to counter buyers' objections. Most importantly, you develop a relationship with the rep that you want to push your line. They are independent entrepreneurs who probably represent too many companies. Your job is to sell them on giving priority to selling your products.

How to Find Sales Reps
There are many ways to find the right Sales Rep for you. Here are some:

- Call buyers you are currently selling and prospective ones. They know all of the Sales Reps, including the new upcoming ones who will have more time for you.
- Ask other Reps in the field. Reps usually network with each other to help find lines in each other's territories.
- Industry Associations will usually give you a list of appropriate Reps. Industry magazines may run ads from Reps looking for lines. Their key employees are good sources for leads.
- Other noncompeting suppliers in your industry can be an

excellent source.

- The Internet will provide you with lists of appropriate Reps to consider. Just Google for them.
- Advertise for the kind of Rep you want. Industry websites and magazines should be the most productive places.
- Putting up signs at trade shows is often a way for Suppliers and Reps to get together. The downside is it usually attracts the newcomers with the least experience.

DIRECT RESPONSE is a way to solicit your potential customer directly without a human calling on them. This is done via mailings, phone calls, or, increasingly, through the Internet. All take know how and, except for the Internet, are expensive. The fastest growth medium is the Internet, but it also has the most competition.

TRADE SHOWS in your industry (if they exist) can be a cost efficient and effective way to reach many of your customers. They, in effect, come to you. However, as a newcomer, it can be difficult to secure a good location and in some cases can be costly. Sales Reps in many instances can be your answer. The experienced ones in many industries have their own booth in prime locations. You can work the booth and save a lot of money by paying a pro rata portion of the booth's cost. The Reps' booth should also draw a good traffic mix of your customers.

WALK-INS are mainly a sales avenue for retail stores or storefront professionals. Potential customers walk in from the street or mall.

PREPARING FOR THE SALE

Preparation and planning are paramount in successful selling. Here are some factors to consider:

Develop a sales strategy by first identifying and prioritizing the types of customers who would most benefit from your service or product. Then discover the characteristics of these customers. Are they primarily large or small? What level of competition do they have with each other? Are they leaders who others will follow? What margins do they insist on? What servicing is required? What are their typical payment terms? Are they customers I can't afford to sell? The list goes on and on.

There is an old saying that is apropos: "Those that fail to plan are planning to fail."

WHAT IS A GOOD SALE

A good sale is one that leads to a reorder (a second sale). The reorder can be aborted due to any one of many dissatisfactions the customer has with their purchased product, i.e., poor quality, didn't live up to expectations, wasn't a fair value proposition, etc.

Another scenario is where you sell your product to a retailer (Wal-Mart, Macy's, etc.) who then resells it to their customer. Many times these retailers enthusiastically purchase products, and their customers disagree with them by not buying it.

The message is don't build inventories or spend anticipated profits on initial sales. You need reorders to have a *good* sale.

Let me tell you a quick story where I failed in this area. I formed a joint venture with a picture frame company, based on my securing licenses for picture frames from a number of major magazines. These magazines included *Time, Sports Illustrated, Golf, Cosmopolitan, Modern Bride, Bon Appetit, Life,* and *Playboy.* The idea was that the consumer would put a picture of their own in the frame which had a clear acetate cover that replicated the magazine's cover. Your doting mate could put you on the cover of *Time* as "Man of the Year" or nominate you as "Golfer of the Year," "Chef of the Year," "Playmate of the Year," and so on.

We were able to work out deals with most of the magazines to get free ads promoting their respective frames and directing the reader to a retailer who was carrying the product. (Good Bootstrapping) Buyers absolutely loved this product. The orders came pouring in. We and our manufacturing partner began to have visions of ourselves as a major, major frame company. Seduced by this dream and by the very positive reactions of the buyers, we cranked up production and waited for the anticipated avalanche of reorders.

What happened next? In a word, nothing. Despite our strong advertising, good retail displays, and retailers' enthusiasm, there was a deafening silence from the marketplace. Our customers—department stores, mass merchandisers, gift stores, catalogue houses, and home-shopping networks alike—all came back to us with exactly the same bad news: the consumer had *absolutely no interest* in buying this product. We wound up taking a bath on our heavy excess inventories, and giving away the profits we could have pocketed from our heavy initial orders. We had a bad sale.

TARGET SPECIFIC ACCOUNTS

After you have prioritized the types of customers you are after, start listing and prioritizing specific accounts. Don't make the list too long. It should be a realistic number that you can effectively call on. The leaders should be a priority. When we were in the game business, we identified the department stores as the priority class of customer. We quickly discovered that Bloomingdale's was a national leader and influencer of other department stores in our category. Buyers from around the country shopped Bloomingdale's when visiting New York. We, therefore, made a major effort to secure that account and service them to death. We built a nice business with them which enabled us to break into many other department stores in all locales.

ZERO IN ON THE RIGHT PEOPLE

Once you've got your key accounts targeted, then find out the name of the person at that company whom you need to sell. Sometimes this is as simple as calling the appropriate office and asking who the lamp buyer is (assuming you're selling lamps). Sometimes, it's harder to find out who's making the buying decisions for your service or product. In some cases, a committee makes these decisions. Assume it's going to take some time to get to the right person (or people) and also assume that it's worth it.

Remember that you're looking for a *decision maker*. A major challenge for sellers today is that, in many cases, they must make their first pitch to a designated buyer who is only authorized to say no. The ability to say yes resides one level higher in the organization—and this is the person you're ultimately trying to reach. However, you have to accomplish this without aggravating the "nay saying," first-screen buyer. (You definitely don't want this person upset with you!) Think of legitimate reasons why you need to go to higher-ups in the organization—and why you'd really appreciate being introduced to those people by the gatekeeper.

If all else fails, run around the gatekeeper. Find a way to get a call in to the higher-up decision maker. When you succeed, you can either ask for an opportunity to make your pitch directly to him or her, or you can ask for something else. One thing that has often worked for me is to inquire, in a sort of peer-to-peer tone, which of their buyers is most appropriate to solicit? You need their advice, especially if your product may fit into several different categories. I've had instances in which the higher-up person directed me to a lower volume department in the store because he or she felt that the buyer in that department was more open to new concepts than the buyer in the higher-volume areas.

If the companies purchase by committee, try to find out the committee members and presell the key ones before their meeting.

UNDERSTAND YOUR TARGET

The next thing that's immensely valuable is to *know everything you possibly can about your prospective customer and buyer*. This is a vital part of preparing for the sale, and it should be ongoing while you're zeroing in on the right person to talk to.

If it's a store, how do they display? Are there clerks who actually sell at the retail counter? How many competing items do they carry? What price points do they carry? What are their profit requirements, and how are they measured? What's their current financial condition? Are they having a good year? What's the long-term trajectory of the company? What kinds of customers do they cater to? Are they leaders or followers? Are they best known for value, price, fashion, or some combination? What special requirements do they have in terms of things like labeling, shipping, packaging, display, advertising mark-downs, quality guarantees, credit terms to their customers, payment terms to you, billing requirements, late-shipment policies, and so on? What's this buyer's personality? What's he or she known for in the trade?

How do you gather all this intelligence? Do your homework, of course! If it's a store, shop the store thoroughly. Talk to the sales clerks.

Take notes. Write down everything that's already in their department that you'd like to sell, and write down what's *not* there that you could provide. If it's a public company, get their most recent annual report (from your broker, from their Web site, or from their investor-relations person). Search them on the Internet. Google the company and the individuals. Talk to other people who sell them. Talk to the receptionists in the company. (In my experience, a bright and under challenged receptionist is almost always a gold mine of information.) Study their ads. Get their catalogs (if they publish them). Read about them and their fiercest competitors in trade publications. Scour their website. Visit trade shows and use these occasions to meet people and ask a lot of questions.

One goal of all this work is to enable you to individualize your call and to be able to speak to your prospective customer's specific needs. Nobody likes to feel that they're getting a "canned" presentation. Conversely, everybody likes to think that they're special enough to deserve special attention from you. They do deserve that special attention! Your preparation telegraphs your competency.

John Korff, the events entrepreneur, says that it's crucial to learn about the people you are going to address: "You have to understand intuitively why someone else should want to do what you want them to do. If there's no logical reason why, it isn't gonna work. That's like firing a shotgun out a window and hoping a duck flies by."

Understand Your Own and Your Competitors' Positions

By this I mean, use what you've learned about the prospect to think again about your own products and services. Which of your customer's problems that you've identified can your products solve? How do the sales histories of your products track with what this buyer needs?

Study all your competitors big and small, and put together a list of the pros and cons of each and how they stack up against your company's offerings. This will sharpen your presentation and prepare you for buyers' questions.

Be sure to do an honest appraisal of your company's products' strengths and weaknesses (which is a very difficult thing to do). This will help you in strategizing your presentation against your competition and focus on improving your pertinent weaknesses.

Selling Approach

Everyone sells differently. There are no right or wrong ways. Practice in most endeavors is a prelude to success. The more sales calls you make, the better you'll be at it. If you're a real beginner, make calls with an experienced sales person. See their approach, but don't necessarily ape them. Develop your own comfortable style. Talk to successful salespeople. Listen to their approaches and sift out the points you feel are important. I can't underestimate how important good listening is to successful selling, and I don't mean hearing. Good listening is a skill that most people do not employ. Listening takes focus. Silence can be your friend. Don't think of what you're going to say next while your prospective customer is speaking. It's okay to have a plan of what topics you are going to talk about, but be prepared to change your order or approach based on what your customer says. Ask good questions and listen, listen, listen.

It has been my experience that most buyers eventually will tell you how to sell them if you listen carefully.

Also keep in mind that most buying decisions are not always made on a rational basis. There are many emotional factors that can do battle with the rational during the purchasing decision, and some of them are unconscious.

WHY BUYERS BUY

Here are a few random factors that I have seen affect a buyer's decision:

- They like you or your company, or they don't like either.
- Their boss told them to buy from you.
- Their customers want your product, or they believe their customers do.
- Your product has appeal because of its quality, price, brand name, warranty, or packaging.
- Your company's offerings are superior to competitors' offerings.
- They trust and have confidence in you.
- Your attention to the detail of the business is excellent. You give them no problems and make life easier for them.
- The previous buyer bought from you.
- They think you are well connected with the management in their company.
- You paid them to buy.
- You are good looking.
- You can help them obtain or maximize their bonus.

There are many more rational and emotional reasons.

SELLING TIPS

- Be persistent. (Don't take rejection personally.)
- Be creative.

- Be patient.
- Be passionate.
- Be proud of selling—remember, buyers need your product.
- Listen, listen, listen. (Think of key questions to ask.)
- Share information.
- Be memorable.
- Be positive—Don't knock others.
- Be prepared to say, "I don't know."
- Make an attractive and comprehensive offer.
- Be prepared to say, "no."
- Ask for the order.
- Follow up with the customer and keep notes on your sales calls.
- Pay attention to detail.
- Build trust—from day one and forever. (See trust list page in Relationship chapter.)
- Never disclose confidential information.
- Budget your time carefully.
- Treat assistants, secretaries, and everyone with respect.
- Treat small customers well.
- Keep looking to solve problems.
- Get customers out of their office.
- Personalize your business relationship.
- Be a team player.
- Become an expert on something: your industry, product, your customer, etc.

In my guest appearances at University Entrepreneurial Classes, one of the most frequently asked questions is "How do you secure an appointment to sell something to a busy person?" Many times this can be a daunting task.

To address this question, I prepared a Tips List and now hand it out to all the classes. This list is reproduced in Appendix 2, and I hope it will trigger some successful ideas for you.

Good selling can offset many other problems the company encounters: unexpected expenses, bad debts, legal fees, increased taxes, higher insurance premiums, etc. These can easily be resolved with more sales.

Selling can also be fun. There is nothing like the rush you get when you secure a big or hard-to-get order.

Happy Selling!

6.
Special Offers to Key Customers

COMPETITION FOR CUSTOMERS in most industries is extremely intense. This is exacerbated if the customer is a large one and your product is not particularly unique or patent protected. Your customers are also in a high pitched battle with their competitors. This can be seen in your everyday life. Look at the competition in cars, retail stores, food stores, homes, computers, music, etc., for your dollar. This extends into the industrial sector and personal services.

Here are some non-cash ideas to help you better compete.

Exclusives. If you have any type of new or unique product and no money to promote it, think of offering a key/large customer an exclusive. The exclusive can be for 30 days to a year with a performance clause for a time specified renewal. When we were in the game business, we would introduce a new game to the leading department store in each major city. We sold them on an exclusive basis for 30 to 60 days in return for their running an ad for our product at their expense. Your exclusive could be narrowed down to a particular channel. For instance, I know of companies that gave Amazon.com an exclusive for all internet selling in return for them giving special promotional pushes for the product. Examples are running 2-day sales or pop-up ads when customers look at a related product (i.e., a wine game when a customer searches for one of their 9,000 wine books).

You could simply give an exclusive to a large retailer for buying it and putting it in all their stores: Radio Shack with 6,000 plus stores, Costco with 500+ stores, Wal-Mart with 3,000+ stores, etc. Exclusives can get you immediate orders, free ads, better position, earlier pay terms, earlier orders, etc. The result is more credibility, more cash, and brand building at no cost.

Better Service. Contrary to popular opinion, most purchasing is not based on the lowest price. Service is a key component in many buying decisions and can take many forms: shorter turnaround in shipping than competitors, customer training on your product features and how to use or sell it, friendly and knowledgeable people manning your phones, customer friendly website, dealing with problems quickly and fairly, admitting, correcting, and paying for mistakes.

One of the key factors of our success in the watch business was our service and special offers. The business was mature, highly competitive, and a *me-too* industry. We entered the industry with a unique novelty approach that featured artwork on the face and a rotating disk with art as the second hand. For instance, our most successful watch was a cute cat with a rotating mouse going around the dial that the cat always just missed catching. These watches were easy for competitors to copy. However, we copyrighted each design and consistently earned money from infringers. We offered two elements that propelled our success.

1. **Special exclusive designs for a low minimum of 200 watches with no premium cost to the buyer**. This was in contrast to large watch manufacturers who asked for a minimum of 10,000 watches. We accomplished our low minimum by working closely with a small Chinese factory, by using standardized parts, and by our willingness to break even on these orders. We knew the profit would come on the re-orders. Our low minimum allowed us to break into the world of Disney, selling to their retail stores, theme parks, and catalog division. All three wanted exclusive merchandise that could only be bought through them. Our small minimums allowed them to test all their ideas without paying a price for mistakes. We were rewarded with large quantity orders for the watches that tested well.

We also rewarded small customers who supported our line with periodic exclusive designs. The result was loyalty and increased business.

2. **Quick turnaround**. This was and is increasingly a key component for small business success and survival. It reduces your cash commitment to inventory and likewise for your customer. It also reduces risk. You need to give a lot of attention and thought on how to realize quick turnaround. We analyzed every component used in a watch and the delivery or manufacturing time of each. We discovered the bottleneck in time replenishment was the unique printed dial on each watch. Every other component was easily available and in stock from many suppliers in China. Fortunately for us, the printed dial was a very low cost component. So we took chances and built up inventories of dials on watches we projected would sell well. The dials cost $.05 each; but in our pricing, we figured it at a $ .20 cost. This gave us the cushion for discarding unused dials.

   We shipped all our watches from China to a public warehouse in Long Island without boxes, which were printed in the U.S. Air freight is a widely competitive business, particularly between UPS and FedEx. Therefore, we eventually flew watches in for $.17 each. We also discovered that the processing of shipments through customs varied greatly by which city they entered. The net result was that we could get watch reorders within two weeks of the order while our competitors' lead time was generally two months. This was a tremendous plus for us with our customers and reduced our cash needs.

Special Terms. Cash strapped businesses with high profit margins should seriously consider additional discounts for immediate or quick payment.

Toy manufacturers usually ship most of their products in the fall. To plan production, particularly with overseas manufacturing, they need orders early in the year. So they successfully offer a special early buy discount to their customers.

Many companies offer volume discounts or rebates. They spell out the discount earned at various volume levels. These discounts can be achieved as you reach the level or can be rebated at the end of the year. This encourages your customers to place more of their business with you rather than sharing with other suppliers.

Private Label. Many products lend themselves to be made under the customer's label rather than your brand. The disadvantage to you is you don't build your brand, and margins are usually lower. The advantages are you don't need to maintain back up inventory, your order lead times are better, and you should get your payments quicker.

Your entire business should *always be customer oriented*. Special offers are particularly effective in building your relationship with a customer and does not drain your cash.

7.
Mentors

ONE OF THE BEST WAYS to start and grow a business is to get expert advice. I'm not referring here to paid consultants, a luxury that most early stage and small companies can't afford. (When you can afford the right ones, by the way, they can be an excellent investment.) Instead, I'm referring here to getting a *mentor* of one kind or another.

I did 27 in depth interviews with successful entrepreneurs in writing my book, *Low Risk, High Reward.* They came in all flavors and sizes. When I asked them what factors they would attribute to their success, the almost unanimous answer was that, early in their career, they had a mentor. Bud Pironti of NSI, a direct response company, was particularly passionate on this subject, and he credits a great deal of his early and continued success to the mentors he's cultivated over the years. (His wife accuses him, jokingly, of "collecting antique men.") Bud stresses that you have to work at these relationships. If you're sincerely humble and solicitous, he says, you'll get back your investment five times over.

What does this mean? It means simple things like saying *thank you* to your mentor and following up to let that person know what happened when you pursued that lead he gave you or when you tried out that idea she suggested a few weeks ago.

Where do you find mentors? The answer is, "Lots of places including unexpected ones." The senior managers of your suppliers may be fertile ground, or perhaps people you've worked with in the past, or college professors, or publishers of industry magazines. Entrepreneurs who own their own businesses are ideal mentors. They're easier to approach than many corporate managers, and they've already been through much of what lies in store for you. Join your local Chamber of Commerce and be active. A mentor-in-waiting can be there.

"Surround yourself with people," entrepreneur Earl Peek advises. "People whom you can call upon for different things. Get someone you can bounce things off of—someone you trust. Get someone with scrapes on his knees, someone who's lost something. The best advice you can get is from someone who's been through something bad."

Again, mentors are everywhere. Think about the people you respect. Can you call upon one of them for advice? Could you build on that relationship over time?

When I talk to young people at business schools who want to start their own companies, I often feel their intense frustration at not having experience and having no way to *get* the experience they need. (You have to have a job to get a job as the old Catch-22 goes.) But I tell them that youth and inexperience are actually great cards for them to play. There are *lots* of experienced, successful business people who are more than willing to help young entrepreneurs if they are approached respectfully. They want to help, and they know that in many cases, teachers learn as much as students.

Another mentoring possibility is SCORE, which is a non-profit, founded in 1964 and funded in large part by the Small Business Administration. The Government chapter gives full details of this free service.

A major source of free advice is a Board of Directors—or the equivalent. I use that qualifier because if you're a small business, you probably don't want to incur the cost of directors' insurance. (This is a must if there are other stockholders involved.) To get around this, call it a "Board of Advisers." But this name change doesn't mean you should take the creation of such a board lightly. No, this board doesn't have the right to get rid of you and hire your successor—as does a formal board of directors—but you should consider it a serious obligation never-theless. Run it in a formal way, and make sure it deals with the same matters as a traditional board of directors. (In most cases, this means policy-level questions rather than operational issues.) Share the numbers. Put together a binder of relevant materials, perhaps including both historical information and forward-looking material, and prepare an agenda. Then send it to the Board well in advance of the meeting. Don't think you are too small for a board.

You can solicit retired executives or entrepreneurs, suppliers or anyone else whom you respect and who might have skills or knowledge that would complement your own for board members. Offer to pay their expenses and—when you can afford it—a nominal fee. (If you make products, think free samples!) Do everything necessary to make this work for you. It's a great discipline, and it can help you focus on tomorrow's problems. Be prepared to take criticism. Remember: that's why you invited them.

TALKING WITH OTHER ENTREPRENEURS

This is an extension of the mentoring approach but more on a peer-to-peer basis. One of the biggest problems in the small company setting is that the CEO/entrepreneur has no one to talk with about troubling issues. Many entrepreneurs aren't comfortable talking about certain issues with employees, and some subjects aren't appropriate for this audience.

I've found talking with other entrepreneurs about my problems to be extremely helpful. It didn't matter if they were in other businesses (which they almost always were). Many issues are common to all small companies. I regularly had lunches or dinners with my entrepreneurial friends, and those relaxed, informal discussions meant a great deal to me. As a result, I always tried to build and maintain these kinds of friendships with people in and outside of my specific industry.

I also found it helpful to join Joe Mancuso's Chief Executives Club, a non-profit organization of small company CEOs dedicated to improving the quality and profitability of their enterprises through personal growth and the sharing of experiences. The organization has chapters in four U.S. cities and nine foreign countries. They run meetings, seminars, and lunches, sometimes featuring high quality guest speakers.

Depending on where you're located, there may be other similar resources available to you. If there aren't, try thinking a little "sideways." Is there an inventors' club in your city? Maybe you'll find some kindred spirits there—or at least, some original thinking. Find people to talk to! Keep Learning!

8.
Business Incubators

IF YOU ARE A START-UP company and you qualify, Incubators can be a fantastic resource for you in your Bootstrapping pursuit of success. They provide the "help of others" part of Bootstrapping and the "limited resources" component of our initial definition of Bootstrapping.

Here is the NBIA (National Business Incubation Association)'s description of Incubators. "Business incubation is a business support process that accelerates the successful development of start-up and fledgling companies by providing entrepreneurs with an array of targeted resources and services. These services are usually developed or orchestrated by incubator management and offered both in the business incubator and through its network of contacts. A business incubator's main goal is to produce successful firms that will leave the program financially viable and freestanding. These incubator graduates have the potential to create jobs, revitalize neighborhoods, commercialize new technologies, and strengthen local and national economies."

Critical to the definition of an Incubator is the provision of management guidance, technical assistance, and consulting tailored to young growing companies. Incubators usually also provide clients access to appropriate rental space and flexible leases, shared basic business services and equipment, technology support services, and assistance in obtaining the financing necessary for company growth.

Incubators are physical plants that primarily house the offices of start-up companies. They will rent you flexible leases, which can allow you to expand or shrink your space quickly. Rents vary by Incubator, but most often are lower than the market rates at the outset. As you grow, you can upgrade to more space. Specifically the Incubator can provide expert advice in areas such as accounting, legal, marketing, and provide more mundane needs such as telephone systems, fax machines, computers, conference rooms, and clean rooms in Tech Incubators. Fees are charged for some of these services and can vary by Incubator. Some Incubators have no fees but want equity in your company.

Although there are few of them, there is growing interest in purely virtual Incubators. They do not have a physical building for clients' offices. Services are provided on what you might call an outpatient basis and/or online. There are no face-to-face interactions. This virtual model extends incubation services in areas that don't have a critical mass of entrepreneurs within a reasonable distance of the Incubator.

A hybrid incubation program is gaining considerable traction where traditional physical Incubators are extending their services to off site companies. This fits well for home-based businesses and companies that already have their own buildings.

Incubators come in many flavors. Some are only for technology companies. Some are for a specialty technology. Some are mixed use while others are service or manufacturing oriented.

Here are some Incubator facts as supplied by Corinne Colbert, Director of Publishing at NBIA.

- There are 1100 to 1200 Incubators in the United States.
- 27% of Incubators have investment funds.
- 70% have links to angel investors.
- The average stay in an Incubator is 33 months.
- About 6% of North American Incubators are for-profit programs.

NBIA estimates that in 2005, North American Incubators assisted more than 27,000 start-up companies that employed more than 100,000 workers and generated annual revenues of more than $17 billion.

Most Incubator tenants accept start-ups, as well as existing companies

Besides the above described advantages afforded to Incubator tenants, some other positives are:

- Networking with other entrepreneurs.
- Getting business from other tenants.
- Getting assistance from specialists in the community to supplement on-site mentors.
- Many Incubators are adding insurance for their tenants.

Be forewarned: it is not easy to get accepted into an Incubator. You need to meet the criteria of the one to which you are applying. For sure, you need to prepare for your interview with a sound, well thought out business plan. These plans do not have to be lengthy dissertations. Succinct and short are good.

No matter the tediousness of the application process, an Incubator acceptance can be a defining moment in your future success.

A study in 1997, funded by the U.S. Economic Development Administration, found that 87% of Incubator graduates were still in business three years after leaving the program. This is considerably higher than start-ups outside of Incubators.

To find the Incubators near you, go to the NBIA website: **www.nbia.org**.

About half of the Incubators belong to NBIA. If you do not see one in your area, then contact NBIA. They will advise you of the ones in your locale that may not be their members.

NBIA's address:
20 E. Circle Drive #37198
Athens, Ohio 45701-3571
Phone: 750-593-4331 | Fax: 740-593-1996

I found the NBIA extremely accommodating.

9.
Universities

PROFESSORS AT SCHOOLS prefer to assign real life problems to their students. At most graduate business schools, they assign students singly or in teams to analyze a real company in their city. The other subject areas like engineering, graphic design, advertising, etc., are also looking for real life assignments for their students.

If you have a product that needs to be engineered, you can approach the professor teaching that subject to ask if students can be assigned to your project. They're usually happy to comply. Most often there is no charge to you. Increasingly, more schools will charge a royalty if it's a product you plan to commercialize. That is still a good deal as there should be no guarantees or up front royalty payment. (A Variable Expense)

We would go to the local design school to get a package for a new product developed. We might give a modest monetary prize to the student with the best design. More importantly, we would put their name on the package . . . great resume builder for the student. You might go to the local college or graduate business school and ask the Entrepreneurship professor if one of their student groups can come up with a business plan for your fledgling company. If you have a legal problem, approach the law school.

One year, we approached the engineering school at a major university to develop a savings bank with all kinds of bells and whistles. We wanted it to keep track of all the money in the bank at any moment, to play a song when money was deposited, to have a tabletop look, etc. For us this was a high tech project. For them it was a piece of cake. They were happy to take on the project as it was a real life situation.

In a recent survey I did with professors of Entrepreneurship, I discovered that a high percentage of them already have programs where teams of students are assigned to assist an existing company in solving its problems. The professors go into the community to find companies who want this help and who will cooperate with the students. They more than welcome companies coming to them to participate in this program. There are some smart young people involved who have a very open minded approach to solving problems and developing ideas. They are not constrained by the past. This is another cost free opportunity for assistance in developing your company.

Whatever your project, you should give serious thought to exploring the schools in your area for help. It can be an excellent cost-free solution. I believe your chances would be higher in schools that have a dominant position in the community. Helping the small guy while offering a good learning experience is a compelling proposition for a teacher.

A bonus for you is that you can find some great interns for your company during the summer months or school year. Some may turn out to be excellent hires.

10.
Relationships and Trust

YOU OFTEN HEAR THAT "it's not what you know but who you know." There is some truth to this. It is human nature to favor people who are friends, who have helped you in the past, who are recommended by friends or by people you respect, etc. That is not to say that they will give you a job, place an order, or do other favors if they think you are incompetent, unprepared, or lack integrity. Good relationships can open doors and can offer you new opportunities. Strong relationships can last a lifetime.

Good relationships are the key to effective networking. Networking is an activity/word bandied about as essential to business success. I would not go that far. Let's first talk about what it is and isn't.

Webster's dictionary defines it as "the developing of contacts or exchanging of information with others in an informal network as to further a career." If furthering a career includes helping you to secure an introduction, get an order, acquire information, etc., then I am okay with it. Networking is not just collecting business cards, no more than starting a business makes you an entrepreneur.

If you do not have this birthright advantage, fear not. You can build your own network of positive relationships by earning them, which makes them more valuable. Relationships are portable. They follow you wherever you go or what job you currently have.

I do not have a list of things you can magically do, and, presto, a good relationship is born. The best way I know to build solid long lasting relationships is to always "Do the Right Thing." Many times you'll be tempted to veer from this maxim, particularly where money is concerned. I like Bill White's comment in his book *From Day One*: "Network more effectively by giving not getting."

This attitude and belief cannot be faked on a sustained basis. You must believe it. Besides helping you in your business, you will sleep better and have a more fulfilling personal and family life.

Doing the right thing comes naturally to many people, and they do it without giving it much thought. However, we live in a complex world, and the right thing may not be clear or be the same for everyone. You can't constantly think of things to say to build trust. Treat all people fairly and with respect, and trust should follow. In building a business it must start from the top and requires thought. Trust fosters, and is mandatory, for good relationships.

Trust takes time to earn but can be lost in a moment. There seem to be generational differences in what constitutes trustful behavior in a business environment. There are many actions that people will call distrustful while others will shrug it off as just business. Trust building is an accumulation of many actions, mostly small ones.

Here is my list of trust building ideas in no particular order.

Listen to people you deal with. (Listening is an acquired skill.)	Do not sell a product you know is bad.
Be honest at all times.	Look people in the eye when you talk to them.
Set an example by your behavior. Give it a lot of thought.	Don't be embarrassed to make a profit.
Admit mistakes right away. (Not easy.)	Don't over promise; resist that temptation.
After admitting a mistake, immediately move to correct it and pay for remedies.	Reprimand people who break their word to you-clearly and decisively.
Pay bills on time. If you can't, call and tell why and when you will pay. (Be sure to give a date you can meet or beat.)	Try to set down specific rules of ethical and moral behavior for company—review them regularly.

Give credit where credit is due.	Keep people informed.
Acknowledge what you don't know. Don't BS.	Specify the relationship you expect.
Push quality. Demand quality.	Problems create opportunities to build trust. Attack problems.
Speak candidly to customers and employees even when it's something you know they don't want to hear but it's in their best interest.	If you receive a check made out to you that doesn't belong to you or are paid too much, the sender should be notified immediately. Don't wait for their auditors to discover the error and contact you.
Keep your promises.	*Thank you* and *please*" can go a long way.
Try to be fair. The attempt is important.	Pay attention to the details of the business.
Don't betray confidential information. Buyers will press you for information about their competition. Don't fall for the trap.	Be prompt in your appointments, your follow-ups, and your promises. Make your deadlines.
Treat *little* people well. (Big ones seem to be easy.) Good assistants eventually get promoted.	Go the extra mile with your customers and employees.
Don't duck or procrastinate dealing with a problem.	Don't knock others.
Answer calls on troublesome issues. Ducking calls creates a new problem, sometimes more onerous than the original one you ducked.	Present solutions, not just problems.
Show respect to every person you deal with no matter their position.	If you don't know the answer to a question, admit it ... then research the answer.

Be knowledgeable about your product, marketplace, new developments, and competition. Share much of this wisdom.	Remember what your parents told you: "Do unto others as you would have them do unto you."
Inform customers of problems as soon as you know and before they find out.	If for whatever reason you can't take on an assignment and give it the attention it deserves … then pass.

I'm sure you can add to the list. Don't expect immediate return or in fact any return for doing the right thing. It should be a way of life for you. However, you'll be surprised at all the good, unexpected things that will come your way. If people trust you, they will have confidence in you. **That will lead to their wanting to do business with you.**

A personal example: at a major trade show we were exhibiting games from the Toy/Game company I co-founded. We had 9 booths, which made us one of the major exhibitors. The largest retailers in the country attended this show as well as thousands of small retailers. The problem for the sales manager or president was if you were working with a small retailer and a major national buyer entered your booth, you wanted to drop or hand off the small buyer you were working with and rush to apply your charms and sales skills on this major buyer. Many people did just that. However, it was not the right thing to do. This happened to me at one show when I was working with a small gift store. A major executive at a large chain walked in. I continued to work with this small retailer and missed the opportunity to personally work the big account.

Now fast forward 10 years. I sold our game company to a major needlework company. After one year, they asked me to be president of the needlework company, which was struggling with an alarming drop in sales. After a review of all their accounts, particularly the ones with big declines, I decided to meet these particular accounts to determine the cause of the sales decline. I phoned the president of one of these, a major national catalog house. In speaking with him, he recognized my name and asked me if I at one time had a game company? When I answered yes, he enthusiastically thanked me for the way I treated him when we first met. It turns out he was the owner of that small gift store that I refused to abandon for the big hitter. I frankly had no memory of the incident. He invited me to come visit his operation. I did and met all his key people who informed me in detail of all the problems they had with our company. We were able to correct these problems to their satisfaction. The end result was a dramatic sales increase that exceeded their previous high point. All this was triggered by doing this one right thing 10 years before. As some would say, "What goes around comes around."

This Relationship chapter overlaps and is intertwined with other chapters like Mentors, Suppliers, Public Relations, and Licensing.

Relationship Building/Networking should become a natural part of your life, requiring no hard thinking. Not only will you be rewarded if you do it the right way, it will be part of your continuous learning. Furthermore, it will cost you nothing.

11.
Pricing for Profit

—————

ONE OF THE MOST IMPORTANT aspects of launching and growing a successful product is correct pricing, one of the major components of profits. The right price gets you an order and maximizes your chances for reorders. The wrong price—on the low side—leaves valuable profits on the table. The wrong price—on the high side—may decrease your orders, your chances for getting reorders, and invite competition.

This may not appear to be a Bootstrap strategy. It is included because a high percentage of businesses do not give enough attention to this important profit element. They too quickly determine price by their costs or by what competition or perceived competition is doing. The result is that profits are left on the table, or more succinctly, you are depriving yourself of precious cash . . . your life blood.

All too often, companies put a selling price on their product or service when they're under some sort of time pressure—for example, when they're dying to rush out there and get some orders. It's not until later that they discover they didn't account for some important costs in that selling price. These costs might include commissions (yes, people forget commissions), extra trade discounts in key markets, displays, servicing, advertising, or whatever. Now comes the trap: in many cases it's very tough to raise prices. (We'll return to this shortly.) So they find themselves stuck with a low-margin item or without the money to run a successful marketing program.

Think of pricing as a balancing act. If you have a unique product, a patentable product, a time advantage, a manufacturing edge, or some other kind of competitive advantage, you can and should get a higher than average margin. At the same time, your high margins may hurt your sales and are very likely to act as a beacon for competitors or knock-offs.

In light of these many calculations, I suggest that you involve all the relevant constituencies within your company in initial pricing discussions. Your accountant may claim that this is his/her domain exclusively. If so, don't let him/her win this argument. Salespeople, production personnel, and even your key customers can provide valuable insights into the pricing decision. You as the manager have to balance these sometimes competing interests and arrive at an appropriate course of action. Notice that I didn't say the "right" course of action. In many cases there's more than one legitimate pricing strategy that can be pursued.

Pricing needs to be revisited regularly. You may find that in order to maintain your margins, you are under pressure to raise your prices. Be forewarned though that you may have major customers who won't accept price increases despite your increased costs. This is particularly true with large quantity buyers. The small company does not have the leverage to demand a justified price increase. I would encourage you—with good humor—to ask for this increase, pointing out your increased costs. If your effort fails and you don't want to hold firm and risk losing the account, you might want to change the product. This change could be accomplished by altering its appearance, adding value to it, changing the package, and even changing the name. Give it a new style number and inform your buyer you are dropping the old one and adding a new one. This can aid a sympathetic buyer who has been instructed by his management to accept no price increases. This way they get around this unfair rule. You should be aware of the fact that if you play hardball and raise your price, you sometimes can win and keep your customer buying the product. Remember it is the buyer's job to keep pressing for the best price. A lot depends on how important the customer's volume is to your business and your mental toughness.

There are four major components to creating profits:

- Selling price
- Cost of product
- Overhead
- Volume

Before you settle on a selling price—especially a price that you may not be able to change easily—here's a list of the selling price and cost of product components you may want to consider. There are also some strategic considerations to weigh before final pricing is done. Not all factors may apply to your product.

SELLING PRICE

1. *Analyze the uniqueness of your product.* What makes your product different? Are you unique and in a hot classification? Or is yours a me-too offering in a declining category which is unlikely to command good margins? Is it a commodity product which again will yield poor margins?
2. *Analyze the barriers to entry behind your product.* What's your sustainable advantage if any? Is it easy for anyone to replicate your business model or copy your products?
3. *Think life span.* The shorter your product's expected life span, the higher your margins should be. Remember that "life spans" apply not only to products but also to whole classes of products.
4. *Know what your market will bear.* Is your product comparable in value to existing products but able to be produced at a lower cost? If so, you might consider pricing close to (or just under) the levels set by your competitors and thereby earning an above-average margin. Alternatively, you could price lower and go for more market share. Whichever way you go, don't make this decision solely on a predetermined margin over your cost. On products with short life spans, what-the-market-will-bear-pricing can be very effective. See Appendix 1, for an example of

how we priced the TV Guide game with a high profit margin. This point and number 3 above were utilized in determining the selling price.

5. *Prepare to be imitated.* Do you anticipate copies or knockoffs? If so, how much time do you have before they enter the fray? You may want to start with a higher margin, and then either lower your margin when competition enters the field or knock yourself off with a lower cost version.

6. *Think longer term.* Will the success of this product lead to successful spin-offs or follow-up sales? If so, you may want to consider selling this original product at minimal or no profit in order to build and capture the after-market or add-on sales.

The classic example is Gillette pricing low for easy razor sales to capture the ongoing blade business, but there are many others. You can forego short-term profits to break into a new channel of distribution with good long-term growth potential, to help your company's image, to gain market share, or to send a strong message to your competitors.

7. *Think strategically.* This is an obvious follow-on to the previous point. Is there some strategy aside from profit that this particular product may help advance? Is this a case where you know you have lots of good (and profitable) follow-up products to put into the pipeline? Will it help you break into a new channel of distribution? Will it help you get a new sought after customer?

COST OF PRODUCT

1. *Determine all your true costs.*
2. *Establish what it takes to be successful in your key markets and with key customers.* Then put a cost on each of these factors. For example:

a. Will you need consumer or trade advertising? If so, to what extent?
b. Will your product require co-op advertising, and if so, what are the standard arrangements in the various markets and customers you're pursuing?
c. Do distributors play a role? If so, what are their margin requirements?
d. What are the margin requirements of target customers in target markets?
e. Is servicing important, and if so, what is your service strategy?
f. Will you be using specialty reps? If so, what commission will you have to pay?
g. What inventory risks will you have to take? How will you handle guaranteed sales, stock balancing, backup stocks, and reorders?
h. What type of packaging will be required?
i. What display (if any) will be needed?
j. What are the standard payment terms in this market?
k. What's the integrity level of this market and of your target customers? (Are you comfortable with those levels?)

3. *Determine the up-front, one-time costs involved in coming to market.* What volume level will be required to recoup these costs at what price?
4. *Examine your cost to acquire a new customer.*
5. *Understand your legal rights and what they may cost you.* For example: if your patent or copyright is infringed upon, will you have the resources needed to start and (if necessary) sustain litigation?
6. *Identify your costs at various volume levels.* Are there dramatic cost savings that come with volume? If so, what strategies and associated costs can you employ to achieve these volume levels?

7. *Examine the "spread."* What are your payments terms from suppliers as opposed to those you give your customers? The cost of money on the spread should be included in your overall costs and prices.

8. *Keep your eye on that license.* If your product is licensed, you probably have both guarantees and royalties to worry about. If the guarantee is high, you may come up short, and you may want to price in light of this potential shortfall.

STRATEGIC

1. *Determine and prioritize the channel of distribution into which you plan to sell.*

2. *Think competition.* You're likely to have competitors and maybe even skilled ones. Will you compete on the basis of product superiority, price, service, quality, advertising, sales coverage, delivery time, or some combination? What costs are associated with this strategy?

3. *Understand the implications of your (limited) finances.* If available finances limit your ability to produce and sell your product, then maybe you should opt for smaller, higher-margin markets. (Yes, there are bragging rights associated with "selling Wal-Mart," but you shouldn't wind up paying for those bragging rights!)

4. *Understand the implications of your (limited) manufacturing capabilities.* Again, if selling Target means you'll sell out your limited run at a relatively low margin, think twice. Shouldn't you look again at those smaller, higher-margin markets?

It has been my observation over the years that not enough time and brain power go into the establishing of your selling price. Maximum profits are good for you and your company's health.

12.
Factors

FACTORS FINANCE $120 BILLION in receivables, yet most small and start-up businesses are not aware of them. Business schools rarely acknowledge them. However, they can alleviate your cash flow problems.

They can loan you or advance you money against your receivables and, in some cases, against your inventory.

In other words, your receivables are an asset that the lender (Factor) purchases.

THE ADVANTAGES OF USING FACTORS:

- You get payment for your invoices within days. This allows you to pay your suppliers on time and thus build up your trust factor with them and to take advantage of their cash discounts. It is a financial tool that speeds your business' cash flow.
- All your costs are variable.
- Factors check the credit of all your customers and would- be ones. Thus, you get more accurate and current information than if you performed this function on your own. Also, more money is saved by eliminating the need to hire a credit checker, and you eliminate your bad debts.
- Factors collect all your receivables. In today's world, the majority of customers like to stall the payment of their bills. Some will not pay until someone calls them for payment. The

Factors have more leverage than you as an individual have. They may represent 50 suppliers of one customer. A number of years ago, one of the biggest retailers in the country was terribly late in paying their bills and in communicating their reasons for so doing. So, the Factor with one stroke told all 50 suppliers to cease shipping this account at once. Needless to say, the CEO of the company immediately got involved, and the checks started flowing again.

- Factors act as insurers of the receivable. If after you ship a customer and the customer goes bankrupt, the factor may be stuck, depending on your contract, not you. This feature can help you sleep better.

- The Factor can take over some of your administrative functions and save you the resultant labor costs. On one of our game companies that was created around a licensed product, the factor supplied us with data on monthly shipments which acted as our Royalty statement. They also provided us with total shipments by territory or account which we used as our Sales Rep commission statements.

- You can get money even though you don't have a good credit rating. The Factor is only interested in your customers' credit rating.

THE DISADVANTAGES OF A FACTOR

- You have a cost for their services, albeit a variable one. Fees can be from 2% to 7% of invoice value. The amount varies based on the credit quality of your customers, the revenue you generate, the health and reputation of your company, and the time it took for your customer to pay the receivable. You should realize that the annualized interest rate in the industry runs 24-36%. The offset of these fees is the savings you generate from some of their advantages. Also, this is often the best of your options; certainly bank loans—if you can get them—are cheaper.

Venture money, if available to you, comes with your giving up equity and possible control.

- Some Factors may alienate your customers with their harsh collection tactics. If this is a problem that you can't resolve with them, then you can take over the collection process.
- You need to thoroughly read the Factoring contract to understand all fees and potential ones.

Once you find the appropriate Factor for you, then all shipments must be approved before you can ship to a customer. Also the Factor will tell you the maximum dollar amount you can ship to a particular customer. The best way to handle this is to supply the Factor with a list of customers you plan to sell. The Factor will, in advance, inform you which companies you can sell and up to what amount. If they don't approve a customer, then you are on your own with that account, and you will get no money for its receivables from the Factor.

There are three general types of Factoring.

1. Regular Factors
2. Asset Based Lenders
3. Purchase order Financing

Regular Factors will advance you money on the receivables (not the purchase orders) of approved credit worthy accounts (in their opinion). This amount is usually 70-90% of your receivables.

Asset Based Lenders will loan you money based on your receivables. Many banks fall into this category. Be aware that this method does not insure you against default of your receivable. Also, you must do your own credit checking and collecting.

Purchase Order Financing is a very small part of the industry. Money is advanced to your manufacturer or exporter, based on your customer's purchase order. The Purchase Order Financer works hand in hand with a Factor, who then takes over the loan when goods are received in a warehouse. This financing method is more for larger companies.

How do you locate the appropriate factor for you? First I would suggest doing an Internet search for Factors in your area. You also could contact your local SCORE (Service Corps of Retired Executives) or SBDC (Small Business Development Centers) chapter. You could also contact your banker if you have one. Another very good source for you is the International Factoring Association. Their website is **www.factoring.org**. Click on Factor Search, fill out their form, and they will match you up with appropriate factors for your needs. All members of the IFA have agreed to adhere to the IFA's strict code of ethics.

You will find many times in your company's life that a factor can be the answer to your cash needs. This is particularly true in a fast growth situation where your money gets tied up in receivables and inventory.

Factoring is an option you should know about and understand.

13.
Suppliers

SUPPLIERS ARE A CRITICAL COMPONENT of your growth and survival. Your approach to suppliers needs to be part of your strategic plan, since almost every company, whether product or service oriented, is dependent on suppliers. Many people seem to get this supplier issue wrong. They feel that because they write the order, they are in the dominant position and can exploit it with unreasonable demands upon their suppliers, including personal perks.

Please let's get this right! You need good and reliable suppliers. When you find them, treat them like gold. I personally don't want gifts from suppliers. For every lunch or dinner they buy me, I want to match it and buy them one. Work as hard on building a supplier relationship as with any other one.

Be loyal to your good ones. They are essential to your good health and your growth. They are a nuanced Bootstrapping strategy.

HOW SUPPLIERS IMPACT YOU

Let's briefly look at all the ways they can impact your company.

- **Quality.** Whether you purchase a component, finished product, or service, suppliers can positively or negatively affect the quality of your product. Higher quality increases customer satisfaction and decreases returns, which add cash to your bottom line.

- **Timeliness.** Their timely deliveries are crucial to how customers view your reliability. Their quick turnaround becomes the key to your minimization of inventory, which in turn translates to less risk of inventory obsolescence and lower cash needs.
- **Competitiveness.** They can keep you competitive and one-up on your competition based on their pricing, quality, reliability, technological breakthroughs, and knowledge of industry trends.
- **Innovation.** They can make major contributions to your new product development. Remember, they live their product more than you do. They are also working to be on the cutting edge of innovation of their product. The good ones will understand your company, its industry, your needs, and help you accordingly in your new idea execution.
- **Finance**. They can be a major and constant source of financing for you. Your payment terms to them can be an important source of money because their extended terms don't usually carry interest. If over a period of time you've proven to be a considerate, loyal, and growing customer, you may be able to tap into your suppliers for additional financing in your growth mode—or if you run into a cash crunch. It may take the form of postponed debt, extended terms on new purchases, a loan, or an investment in your company . . . all of which improve your cash position.

Jerry Shafir, the founder of Kettle Cuisine, a quality soup maker, used his suppliers as a key element in his growth. After years of bootstrapping, his company gained traction but could not get the cash they needed to grow. Jerry went to his key suppliers for extended payment terms, and they gave it to him. This was a key factor in his growth to become a major player in the soup industry, by allowing him to invest in state of the art soup making equipment. The suppliers supported Jerry because he gained their trust as an honest, ethical, hardworking, and passionate individual.

To maximize the benefits your suppliers can deliver to you, it is important that you be open with them. Include them in some of your strategy meetings, invite them to break bread, visit their offices, and invite them to meetings with your people, including companywide ones or office parties or picnics. In other words, work hard to build a good relationship with them.

Having said how valuable and important a supplier can be to you, I'll now say that you should not be a patsy. You can be a demanding customer—just be *fair*. State your quality and time needs clearly. Hold your suppliers to their agreements. Make sure they stay competitive. Tell them you never expect to pay higher prices than other purchasers.

Let them know that you are there for the long term as long as they perform and can keep pace with your growth. There are times you need to replace a supplier because you have outgrown them and they can't perform to your new expectation. Before dropping them, however, I would try to educate them or help them change to keep up with you. Failing that, you might be able to throw them some bones in the hope that over time they can change and grow to meet the needs of your new business model.

It's not prudent to rely on one supplier. If that supplier has a strike or a fire, you don't want to be in a position where you'd be shut down too. So develop a second or multiple suppliers and don't be embarrassed to tell your key supplier that you're doing so. They will appreciate your honesty. If they are savvy, they'll also know you need backup suppliers on key products or services if you are to raise money. The lenders are sure to ask this question.

HOW TO BE A VALUED CUSTOMER

These ideas assume, of course, that you are a customer that somebody out there wants. Don't take this for granted! In order to be a valued customer to your suppliers, here are a few good things you should do:

- **Pay your bills on time.** For the sake of emphasis, I'll repeat this one: *Pay your bills on time!* You can negotiate for favorable payment terms before you place an order, but once the order is placed, don't renege or attempt to change the rules.

  Always pay on time. If for some reason you can't, call up your suppliers and tell them why, and then tell them when you will pay. Don't play games with suppliers' cash. You'll be absolutely amazed at the goodwill and benefits you will earn by observing this simple rule.

  Don't let your bookkeeper or comptroller think he or she is a hero if he/she succeeds in stalling payments. In fact, I personally would come down hard on anybody who tries to do that as a general rule. My question to that person would be, "Who do you think is going to get deliveries when there is a shortage of product? The prompt payer or the staller?" Personally, I feel that deliberately stalling supplier payments is stealing.

- **Provide adequate lead times.** Try to give suppliers as much lead time as possible on your orders. Unless there's a good competitive reason not to, share with them your *honest* projections of your needs, and then keep them abreast of any significant changes in that estimation. In developing your lead times, try to be knowledgeable about your supplier's production methods and needs.

- **Share information.** Keep your good suppliers aware of what's going on in your company. Tell them about changes in key personnel, new products, special promotions, new markets, and so on. Many times, you'll find that good suppliers can be helpful to you in developing new business.

Developing good suppliers and dealing with them effectively is not a complicated process. Tell them of your needs and standards, treat them fairly, be demanding, be loyal, be communicative, and *pay them on time.*

14.
Testing the Waters

OFTENTIMES ENTREPRENEURS—blinded by their belief in their new product idea which is reinforced by their loved ones—lunge full force forward in the production and marketing of their can't miss product. They will invest in some or all of an optimistic quantity, expensive brochures, displays, molds, public relations campaign, advertising, and more. All this, based on their personal beliefs. Optimism and confidence are valuable traits for an entrepreneur, but sometimes they are misguided and extremely costly. No one is smart enough to know in advance how consumers and the market will react to their new product. Large companies can absorb a failed product. Small company failures can be fatal.

Small companies don't have the money to do the extensive research and testing, as do their larger brethren. Here are some (almost) cash free ideas to test your new product concepts in advance of your cash commitment to its success.

- First, accurately research the cost of your total product or service and the costs to bring it to market. Then determine your selling price. Knowing this will make the following steps more realistic.
- Make an inexpensive prototype or good drawings and show them to select potential customers and ask them if they would buy it at the price determined.

You will get a variety of answers from yes to no (with or without emphasis) to maybe or yes, if you would change this or that. If there is strong feeling one way or another, it can point you to the right action. If every buyer said they wouldn't buy it, I would probably abort or go back to the drawing board to re-invent it. You should know that many buyers are flattered that you are soliciting their input. If they are affirmative or you incorporate some of their suggestions, they often take some ownership in the product and feel obligated to buy it when ready.

The most dramatic example of this type of testing for me was when we secured the license to market a TV Trivia Game from *TV Guide*. This was at the time Trivial Pursuit was beginning to become a phenomenon. We felt we had a short window and certainly didn't know how we would fare. We quickly made a good package prototype and brought it to the Toy Fair along with a copy of the cost free ads we would be running in TV Guide. (We received these free ads as part of our license agreement by offering a higher royalty.) When we presented our prototype in February, we promised a May delivery and asked for orders. Lo and behold, we received over $2,000,000 in advance orders from this one prototype. In all fairness, this outcome was also due to our good reputation in the industry. (Buyers trusted we would keep our word.) The fact the ads were offered with customer's names and that trivia games were becoming a hot category made it irresistible to buyers.

However, if at the annual industry Toy Fair, all the key customers had shown no interest, we would have aborted the entire project. This would have saved us a good deal of money as we had not yet developed the 6,000 questions needed, nor the final artwork, and certainly no inventory or sales materials. This would be money saved to use for another product.

SOME TESTING IDEAS

- Focus Groups are used by many companies to judge the viability of their idea. This process can be done by professionals for a fee or you can assemble your own group gratis. (Don't use family or friends.) I do not put great faith in focus groups as I think it is different asking someone if they will buy something or actually reaching in their pocket for cash and handing it to you. They can, however, point you to a possibly extreme mistake.

- Many companies initially introduce a product nationally or internationally. However, for us small biz folks, we should test in small controlled areas first. This reduces risk; but just as important, you learn from the effort. Nobody can anticipate everything. Your testing-induced knowledge can lead you to important modifications of your product or offer. These changes can be the difference between success and failure.

- Talk to the salespeople who will be selling your product. You should know which of them are honest sounding boards. Many sales people tend to tell you what they think you want to hear.

- The Direct Mail industry and the 1-800 TV ads generate huge sales of product. However, they never invest heavily in product until they *know* it will be successful. This they do by testing. If a mailer has a list of 20,000,000 potential customers, the test offering might be to 50,000. If that works, they might test 500,000. If all these early tests work, then they will do the entire mailing list.

- The Internet allows you to test your product in the same way.

- Home Shopping Networks. When we were in the watch business, we always tried to introduce our new offerings first to the Home Shopping Networks, HSN and QVC. Aside from their volume potential, they were a perfect testing vehicle for us. We knew immediately which watches were the winners and losers. This fantastic knowledge was not only at no cost, but we made a profit.

- If your product is sold through a retail store, talk to the retail sales clerks who are selling your product. They are a gold mine of information. Here is my Wal-Mart story, where I visited a few of their stores regularly to see how they were doing with my rotating disk watches. Watches are sold in the jewelry department behind a counter with a sales clerk in attendance all the time. I would visit these stores mid morning when the traffic was at its lightest.

The sales clerks were usually flattered to have the president of a company talk to them. (Albeit a small company) I would ask lots of questions like why is this watch displayed where it is? What type of watches sell best? Do more women or men buy my particular type watches? As I got to know them through follow up visits, I would venture questions about other company's watches, like what were the best and worst selling watches in the department? I received good answers.

One day I happened to ask the sales lady if her customers requested any particular subjects for our topic oriented watches? She said, as a matter of fact, a number of times customers came in and asked if we had the Cat and Mouse watch. This was the first watch we made, and it was subsequently copied by someone who sold it on TV. This was now two years later. I then visited other Wal-Mart stores and asked the sales clerks the pointed question, "Do your customers ever ask for the Cat and Mouse watch?" The answer in all instances was yes.

Armed with this information, I contacted our buyer at Wal-Mart headquarters in Bentonville, Arkansas, and relayed the information about the cat and mouse watch requests in her stores. She verified my findings and proceeded to place an order for our Cat and Mouse watch for most of her stores.

Over the years, I have had consistent positive feedback, leading to good things for our company by visiting the retail sales clerks. They are the direct link with the consumer who buys your product. Often, they know much more than the higher paid corporate buyer who spends most of his or her time behind a desk. A number of new product ideas have emanated from this source. The only investment for me was my time.

If you are a service company, you should strive to have regular dialogue with those who use your product, not just its buyers. Those are the ones in the trenches who know all the pro's and con's of your product and could probably tell you how to improve it.

Remember, talking to people costs nothing, and you have no obligation to follow the advice you get. However, if you ask good questions and are a *good listener*, you can save yourself lots of money and discover new actionable ideas.

15.
Licensing

NORMALLY THE SUBJECT OF LICENSING would not appear in a Bootstrapping context because there usually is an up-front cash payment and a guarantee associated with securing a license. These two factors can be substantial with a high visibility license, such as Mickey Mouse, NFL football, Nike, Armani, etc. However, I bring it up here for two reasons:

1. In the early stages of your business, a good license offers advantages as well as potential pitfalls. An early understanding of the how-to's of licensing can aid you in identifying license opportunities and how to capitalize on them.

2. I believe there are some niche licenses in the early stages of your company where no cash up-front is required and your only payments are royalties (a Variable Expense). One example of this was in our second year in the watch business (A mature industry with many large companies). We secured the watch license for the Wizard of Oz and Gone with the Wind. We paid no up-front monies, only a royalty on shipments. It was a not-in-demand license; we had good marketing experience in other industries; most of all, our plan to sell to a niche market (Direct Response Companies and Collectibles) was well received. We were successful and gained needed credibility in a new field for us. This led us to eventually secure licenses for Elvis Presley, the NFL, NASCAR, Precious Moments, and others. Our

concentration on untapped watch markets and our unique watches powered our success.

Here is a short tutorial on the license industry.

First, *Licensing* is the process whereby one company uses the trademark, property, or brand name of another company in return for some form of compensation. In most cases, the licensor grants the licensee some sort of exclusivity—perhaps geographical, perhaps by product, perhaps by distribution channel. Most often, the compensation involves some sort of up-front fee and a percentage of sales (a *royalty*).

There's an amazing range of products for which licenses are issued. They include, for example, limited-run automobiles, perfume, plates, cereals, vitamins, toys, clothing, jewelry, and beverages. The number and volume of licensed products seems to grow each year. The total volume at retail for the year ending 2007 was $180,000,000,000, according to LIMA, the industry association.

Why go this route? There are at least seven good reasons:

- *More Credibility in selling into established distribution channels.* This is particularly true for young companies. The right name of the license on your product will get you in the front door with your target customer. If this particular licensor's goods have performed well in this distribution channel in the past, your product is less risky for this retailer. Your potential customer may not have heard of you, but they most likely will have heard of your licensor.

- *Competitive Advantage.* A license takes your product out of the commodity class—it's not just a watch; it's a Mickey Mouse watch—and simultaneously protects your product from being knocked off. This, in turn, means that you can usually build and maintain higher profit margins despite the higher selling price that is necessitated by the pass-along of royalty charges.

- *Better Sell-In.* In many situations, a specific license will open the door to sell a new account or to sell more products to an existing account.
- *Better Sell-Through.* Because consumers recognize and (hopefully) like this brand or image you've licensed, they will pull your product through the distribution channels. This will lead to the reorders that will keep you in business.
- *Better products.* In some cases, a licensed process or technology permits the licensee to make a more valuable product and to get into markets that he or she otherwise couldn't penetrate.
- *Access to capital.* A good license will assist you in getting capital (whether invested or loaned). Smart "money people" know the value of an appropriate license.
- *More company value, more quickly.* A successful licensed product builds the value of your company which will help you if you sell, go public, or merge.

In light of all these benefits, licensing may sound like a gold mine. In many ways it is. However, as in all other realms of business, there are questions to be answered and obstacles to be overcome on the road to success.

The first question you need to answer, *honestly*, is whether your product is good and whether there is a demand for it. Just as great advertising can't sustain an inferior product indefinitely, a good license can't rescue a bad product. Don't pay somebody else money for the right to produce a product that nobody wants. As licensing consultant Stu Seltzer says, "Licensing can make a good product great . . . but it cannot make a bad product good."

The second thing to be aware of is that licensing is a competitive field. Lots of people want to use Mickey Mouse's face. As a result, Disney can afford to be choosy and expensive—and they are.

What does a potential licensor want to see when he looks at you? One major licensor, Peter Van Raalte, former VP of Turner

Entertainment and Scholastic Entertainment, Inc., told me that he looks for six things when evaluating a potential licensee:

- Distribution
- Distribution
- Distribution
- Creativity and quality
- Appropriate positioning of the property
- Financial responsibility

In my experience, all licensors put an overwhelming emphasis on distribution. They are granting you a valuable right in the expectation that you can get enough orders in markets where they think their products should be available. This means that you're likely to be asked about your distribution capability. Although this is, in many cases, an obstacle, it may also be an opportunity. Licensors with strong properties are increasingly inclined to award licenses by *channel of distribution*. If your company is new and inhabits an unusual niche— say downloadable Internet games—a channel-specific license may present a special opportunity.

When licensors evaluate you as a potential licensee, they will check your references with retailers and other licensors (if any). They will want to know your market strategy, point-of-product differences, quality, and on-time delivery record; and they will want reassurances that you have the financial strength to do a good job with the property. Finally, they may want to explore whether your corporate philosophy and culture fit well with their own.

Looking at licensing from the other end of the telescope: As a licensee, you have to choose your licensed product with care. Here are some sensible questions to ask:

- Does this relate to the consumer of my product? (Do I want a Big Bird license for my watch company if I'm convinced that most preschoolers can't tell time and don't wear watches?)

- Is this a good fit with my product? (If I make farm implements, how valuable is a ready-to-wear designer brand name?)
- Do the buyers in my major channels of distribution think highly of this license? (How hard will they work for it if they don't?)
- Can I afford the guarantee, advance payment, and other commitments related to this product? Are the royalties too high for the product? Is this license strong enough to make up for the higher retail price it will have to command?
- Is this a license I want to put resources into and build for the long term, or is its value short term or tactical—e.g., to sell one account or one channel of distribution?
- What's the reputation of the licensor? Will they renew my contract if I do a good job? Will they award too many licenses to competitors in my category? What type of artwork will they provide and at what cost? How long is their approval process? Is their contract fair, and can I live with it? Can I trust them?
- What is the licensor's policy when major national retailers come to the licensor to give them exclusive product? Will they work through their licensee, or will they do a direct deal and circumvent the licensee? Most licensing contracts are non-exclusive and would therefore allow the licensor to make these deals directly with a retailer.

Contracts deserve a closer look. While every licensing relationship is different, here are some of the topics that will come up in negotiations for a license:

- *Territory covered.* Could be by country, geographical, distribution channel or even by specific accounts.
- *Products to be covered.* You, the licensee, should try to keep it broad. If you make watches, you want the contract to say timepieces. This wording will cover you on pocket watches, clocks, etc.

- *Rates of royalty.* Usually not very negotiable unless you have a product that is not replicated. As an early stage company, you might want to think of offering a higher royalty for no upfront costs or other goodies that are important to you.
- *Length of contract.* You want longer; licensor wants shorter. You should strive for automatic renewals if certain targets are met.
- *Guarantees.* Again, Licensee and Licensor are on opposite sides of the fence. Negotiate . . . Sell.
- *Promotional Dollars.* The Licensor will usually ask you to commit for an amount of money to be spent on their licensed product. You want to stay away from high specific amounts. Your pubic relations competency can be worth more than paid ads. How will that be measured?
- *Advances.* Licensor will almost always ask for a check upon signing. If you are only licensed for a niche, that should be an argument for lower or no advance. As mentioned earlier, you could trade higher royalty for no advance. I personally always used my small company status as an asset, which gave us more focus, flexibility, passion, hunger to succeed, etc. We also needed the cash flow more than the rich licensor. Advanced with humor, it often worked.
- *Exclusivity.* Many licensors give out too many licenses for the same category. This negates one of your prime reasons for taking on the license. Carefully assess this point.

As always, doing your homework is important. Before signing a license, check out other licensees about their experience working with this licensor. The Licensor will supply you with their list of licensees. Talk to potential customers. Develop a marketing plan before your first meeting, etc. The licensing business has become more sophisticated over the years, so put effort into your presentation and be professional.

Most importantly, when you get that first license, bust your butt to make it a success. The word spreads fast among licensors on who are the new rising stars. You want to be one of them.

The best place to contact for information on the licensing industry is:

International Licensing Industry Merchandisers Association (LIMA)
350 Fifth Avenue, Suite 4019
New York, NY 10118
Phone 212-244-1944
Fax 212-563-6552
www.licensing.org

16.
Franchising

FRANCHISING IS A TYPE OF business arrangement that lies somewhere between buying a business and starting your own. It involves an agreement between a Franchisor (Burger King, Subway, Mail Boxes etc,) and you, the individual business person, called the Franchisee.

The Franchisor offers their established corporate brand name, experience, expertise, training, support, and proven methodology to the Franchisee. In return, the Franchisee pays an upfront fee and continuing royalties.

I bring Franchising up in the Bootstrapping context as it almost completely solves the experience/know-how part of the limited resources equation. As to the cost part, many Franchises will be clearly out of most start-ups' reach. However, the franchising industry is so big and diverse that many have a relatively low initial cost. Recently *Entrepreneur* magazine had an article on 80+ Franchises that required an initial cost of $25,000 or less. (Entrepreneur.com)

There are over 2,500 Franchises in the country in 90 different industries, employing 21,000,000 people. There are many and diverse categories of businesses available for Franchising. A partial list, as seen on entrepreneur.com, is Automotive, Business Services, Children's Products & Services, Education Financial Services, Food, Health Care, Home Improvement, Hotels & Motels, Maintenance, Personal Care, Pets, Recreation, Service & Tech businesses, and more every year.

Jeffrey Tannenbaum, the former *Wall Street Journal's* expert on Franchising, described Franchising as a mixed bag. He said, "For many people becoming a franchisee is the shortcut to prosperity, but for others, it is the shortcut to hell."

Let's look at the pros and cons of Franchising.

ADVANTAGES

- *Allows you to be in your own business* with a limited knowledge of the industry and of running a business. You get the advantage of the Franchisor's proven track record of success, their training, their operating methods, their suppliers, their credibility, their ongoing support, etc.
- Some major *risks* of business failure are reduced.
- *Quick start* to get your business operational. Every facet of starting and running the business is provided to you. An entrepreneur, starting on his or her own, would take considerably longer to begin.
- *Expansion*: If you become successful, you can expand quite rapidly through the expertise and cooperation of the Franchisor. They are anxious to discover successful operators who have proven they have what it takes to grow. Sometimes the Franchisor will block your expansion plans, despite your proven success. If this happens, you can draw inspiration from Sam Walton, the founder of Wal-Mart. Sam's initial entry to retailing was as a Franchisee for the Ben Franklin 5 & 10 Cent stores. He followed their formula and added his creativity and work ethic to become a leading franchisee. He started to expand in neighboring Arkansas towns. Early on, Sam spotted the advent of retail discount stores. He approached the Ben Franklin management to let him pioneer a discount store under their umbrella. They summarily dismissed him, and Wal-Mart was born. Little did the Ben Franklin management realize how profoundly they would affect retail history.
- *Due Diligence*: Franchising is a highly regulated business. By law, every potential Franchisee upon asking must be provided with a

Franchise Disclosure Document from the Franchisor. This will give you details of the arrangement with Franchisees, financial strength of Franchisors, their list of existing Franchisees, and, in many cases, lists of past Franchisees. You want to know everything you can about your potential partner.

- *Training* is provided to you and to your employees. The learning curve of running a business is accelerated.
- In most cases *Advertising and Marketing* of the brand is provided. In some cases, you may be required to contribute to the costs of it.
- *Territory:* You are assigned an exclusive Franchise for a specified geographic area. No one else can use your brand in this defined area. This provision should be specifically spelled out in the contract.

DISADVANTAGES

- *Lack of Control:* You don't have the independence of an owner of a business. The Franchisor requires you to strictly follow their rules and to use their systems. Changes require approval. You are also limited in where to buy your supplies, how to advertise, which products you can and cannot offer, volume goals, etc. The arrangement can be frustrating for a creative personality.
- *Costs* can be high, both the initial fee and ongoing royalties. However, costs are never to be considered in a vacuum. They need to be measured against the profits you create.
- *Royalties* are paid on volume and not on profits in most instances. This is usually not a great arrangement as one party can lose money while the other profits. Their interests are not aligned even though it is a partnership.
- *Inequality:* It is an unequal partnership. The Franchisor has much more power. If the Franchisor does not deliver on their support promises, you may not have much recourse, as most

contracts favor the Franchisor. Also, you may not have the money to pursue your expensive legal options.

- *Selling the company* may be difficult. Let's say you've been successful over the years in building the franchise and want to now retire or change your lifestyle. In an independent business, you are completely free to sell to anyone at any price you desire. This is not necessarily so for a Franchisee. Some contracts won't allow you to sell, or you can only sell back to the Franchisor. This might not allow you to get a fair price. So, you should try to address this issue in your original contract.

WHERE TO GET HELP

In determining if Franchising is for you and which ones best fit your pocketbook and passion, you can go to the following sources:

- *Google:* Just search for Franchising, and you will get enough sources to look at to keep you busy for a lifetime.
- **Entrepreneur.com** is the website of *Entrepreneur* magazine which puts out a yearly issue of the top 500 Franchises. They offer a list by category and by costs. You can get a brief outline of each Franchisor and their website for more information.
- *FTC:* The Federal Trade Commission is the government regulatory body for the Franchising industry. The FTC website is www.ftc.gov. They are located in Washington, DC, and their phone number is 202-326-2222.
- *The American Franchising Association* (AFA) is an industry association located in Washington, DC. They have lots of information about Franchisors and the industry. Their website is **www.franchise.org**. Phone number is 202-628-8000.
- *www.bestfranchiseopportunities.com.* This website lists a multitude of Franchising opportunities with descriptions of each. You can check up to 10 of them, and with one click, your request for more information goes out to each company. I found that I

received the same day replies from all that I clicked, with phone calls from them starting the next day.

- *www.Inc.com* is the website for *Inc.* magazine, the publication for entrepreneurs. They have extensive information about Franchising and lists of questions to ask a potential Franchisor.

With a lot of due diligence, Franchising may be the low risk, low cost way to become your own boss.

17.
Converting Fixed Costs to Variable Costs

A *Fixed Cost* IS ONE THAT your business incurs whether or not it makes any sales. An example is rent: it has to be paid every month whether or not you're generating any income, and it's the same every month.

A *Variable Cost*, by contrast, is incurred only when you make a sale. A Variable cost usually varies directly with the amount of the sale. A commissioned salesperson, for example, is a Variable Cost. If the person is getting paid 10 percent of sales, and the sales for a given month are $25,000, then that person gets $2,500 in commissions. If sales drop to $1,000, then the commission drops to $100.

Maximizing variable expenses reduces the amount of capital you'll need to handle overheads and operating expenses in slow selling periods. A low monthly Fixed Expense ensures that you'll get to breakeven (and even profits) faster. As a general rule, investments in overhead should be made only when you have a degree of certainty about the product and when customer demand is (1) strong and (2) well understood.

Here are some examples of Fixed Costs that can be converted to Variable:

- **Sales.** Instead of hiring full-time salespeople and getting burdened with their weekly or monthly wages, go with independent sales representatives (reps) who will work on a percentage basis. You also pay none of their expenses. Ineffective reps are easier and less costly to replace than full-time salespeople, and they don't present the burden of benefits, which can run as high as 30 percent of the salary of a full-time employee. Reps should have strong relationships with customers in their territory, which can translate into quick access and orders. Reps can specialize in an industry, work geographically, or sell to specific accounts.

- **The factory.** You don't have to own a factory just because you want to produce, assemble, store, ship, and build your product. Contract manufacturers are happy to do all or some of the above for you. (Find them on search engines or the yellow pages.) They charge either for the space you take up and/or the functions you ask them to do. Most will work out a deal with you to charge a percentage of your billing. This then makes this a variable expense. Either way, this represents a huge saving in fixed and operating costs. Contract manufacturers also maintain insurance on your goods in their possession. They cover the cost of their employees' benefits. Yes, there are some downsides—including the fact that you may have to vie with their other customers for priority. Here persuasion and salesmanship are your best weapons. As soon as your volume warrants it, allocate a full-time person to cultivate the relationship with your "extended factory." At some point, you may even want to position your employee on their premises for more control (and reduced risk).

You may have the type of product that would permit you to pay another manufacturer to make it for you under your brand. (This would be their "private label.") Products like beer, liquor, drugs, and computers are often made under this kind of arrangement.

- **Administration.** Guess what? Your billing, sales reports, commission statements, royalty statements, inventory reports, and aging reports can also be done on a percentage basis by your contract manufacturer. Of course, the more functions you outsource, the higher your percentage payment will be. But remember: everything that you're outsourcing is a function that you're not hiring a salaried body to perform. And it's not just bodies either. Why should you pay for the latest computers and software to run them—especially if they'll only be used for a small fraction of the working day? Pay someone else to worry about that. You also don't have to pay the price of obsolescence which can be very high in the world of computers. Your customers will have absolutely no idea that these functions are being outsourced. (They probably wouldn't care if they did know.) And your company takes on the aura of a well-established business from the outset. There are companies that specialize in doing all the administration for you.

- **Inventors/Designers.** You can get quality people to invent, develop, and/or design product for you on a percentage of the products' billing . . . in other words on a variable expense basis. Many will want to work on up front fees only. (Fixed Expense) Salesmanship on your part can get them to charge your way. (A Variable Expense) If they are sold on your company, you personally, or the product, they are more likely to comply with your wishes. Sometimes a compromise is required where you pay a modest up front fee and a modest percentage on sales of the product.

- **Public Relations.** This is a special section in itself, but there are some Public Relations firms that will charge on performance. Usually, they only work on a fee basis. A performance-based agreement (Variable Expense) should be carefully spelled out . . . Specific accomplishments and their exact costs. Usually in start-up or early stage companies, the principals need to do their own Public Relations. Some of the ways were spelled out in the Public Relations section earlier in this book.

Converting Fixed to Variable Costs is a major way to reduce your need for money. It could also be the difference between success and failure for young companies. Every fixed cost should be scrutinized for conversion to a Variable Cost. You might be surprised how many can be converted.

As you grow your company, there may come a time when the company volume reaches a level where the Fixed cost is less expensive than a Variable one. However, before you switch, make sure you can maintain this high volume. Do not switch on the basis of sales projections or a one-time up tick.

18.
Outsourcing

OUTSOURCING IN RECENT YEARS has gotten a bad name from some in the media and from politicians, looking to get votes.

Outsourcing is basically purchasing your product, components, or services from an outside party. This is in lieu of you performing those functions. The common view is that these products and services are purchased only from foreign suppliers. However, a significant amount is done by domestic suppliers who do not ship American jobs overseas—as many in the media profess.

The outspoken critics of outsourcing claim it takes away American jobs. Many go so far as to say it is unpatriotic for a business to outsource to foreign suppliers. Bah, Humbug.

Outsourcing is not a new phenomenon. It has been in existence since businesses began. If it were outlawed, the country that adopted it would be plunged into a serious depression. Many businesses would fail, and consumers' prices would skyrocket.

Outsourcing can be a Fixed or Variable cost. If the cost is based on volume or space used, it is a Variable. If cost is set at a fixed amount, based on the function provided, it is Fixed. In most cases outsourcing is variable.

Let's look at the positives of outsourcing. Many products or services can be made by others at lower prices and higher quality. This could be the determining factor in survival for many companies. From my own experience, I had an idea for a novelty watch and decided to start a watch company. The watch industry was very mature and competitive.

It would be impossible to even get started in the U.S. if you did not purchase your watches from overseas.

There is a high labor component in the manufacture of watches. If you choose to make them yourself, there is a huge capital investment. There are about four companies in the world that can make the movements. So, a new company like ours—by using outsourcing—got into the watch business with zero investment. Our only fixed cost was in the development of the watch. This cost us about $200 per watch style, using freelance artists who were not on our payroll.

The watches were made in China and were shipped to a public warehouse within a 45-minute drive from our office. This warehouse put the watches in our boxes, stored the watches, and shipped to our customers. They also did our computer work and in fact billed our customer as soon as the order was shipped with all invoice payments going to us. All of this was billed on a percentage of the value of the invoice. (A Variable Expense)

Our sales were outsourced by using Sales Reps. At least 50% of my time was spent in direct selling of our products.

We were successful and within four years, we had 15 employees. That's 15 new jobs. The fact is most new job creation in the United States comes from Small Business.

Almost everything can be outsourced. We spoke of some functions like Sales, Manufacturing, and Administration in our Variable Cost section. However, outsourcing eliminates the need and *cost* to perform these functions. Thus, less money you need to raise.

Outsourcing relieves the entrepreneur of his/her knowledge deficiencies by shifting this responsibility to the supplier.

Outsourcing is a key ingredient in our standard of living as reflected in lower prices of consumer products.

One of the criticisms of outsourcing is that you lose control by utilizing it. This is true to a certain extent as your supplier is an independent company and does do work for other people. You can be sure that all companies using your supplier want their orders shipped first, but there are many ways to overcome this seemingly negative:

First always pay your suppliers on time. You would be shocked at how much service and goodwill this gets you.

You need to establish a strong relationship with your key suppliers, both management and employees working on your account. There was a more in depth exploration of Suppliers earlier in the book.

My experiences have mostly been good with suppliers. In fact, I think the control issue is bogus in most cases, which I learned the hard way. When we were in the game business, we sold our small company to a stock exchange company who promptly built us a 70,000 square foot facility. Part of the plant was used to manufacture wood games, which were about 15% of our business but 98% of our headaches. We had OSHA laws to contend with and were completely at the mercy of our plant manager. I had no clue about the manufacturing of wood products. After some exploring, I turned to Taiwan where we found a reliable supplier who could deliver the products at a cheaper price than we could make it, but most importantly, of a much better quality. This stopped all the customer complaints. Also, the outsourcing suppliers are in a very competitive situation. This taught me that my control in outsourcing is that if a supplier does not perform to our agreed to terms, I can switch suppliers at no significant cost. In my own manufacturing, I can switch plant managers but would have to endure a learning curve and still be dependent on one person. Every switch is expensive. Here's an example of domestic outsourcing I experienced:

When the Rubik's Cube puzzle took America by storm, it created an opportunity to produce a solution book for this most difficult puzzle. For some reason, Ideal—the company marketing the Rubik's Cube—didn't offer such a book. Quickly, two book companies created solution books that eventually reached the top of the New York Times best-seller list.

By this time, I already had experience as a partner in a toy/game company. I was shopping the game department in Macy's and noticed a big display of Rubik's Cube solution books adjacent to the cubes. Back then, and to some extent today, the idea of selling a book outside the book department was a radical idea.

However, the Macy's book department was adjacent to the adult game department, and the buyer—whom I knew, and who was a very creative and entrepreneurial type—bought for both departments. As I surveyed the game department, I spotted the buyer and asked her how the solution books were selling. She told me the books were doing great. In fact, her impression was that for every three cubes that were sold, two books were sold.

I immediately bought the small paperback book, which retailed for $2.00. I then called the book publisher to inquire about buying the books in quantity to resell them into the toy field so that toy retailers could sell them adjacent to their cubes, a la Macy's.

Book publishers sell books on a "guaranteed sale" basis, which means the retailer can return all unsold books for credit. To minimize their exposure in this potentially risky relationship, the publishers work on high margins and give retailers lower than average profit margins as compared to non-guaranteed sale products. Knowing this, I asked the publisher to sell me the book for 50 cents with the idea of reselling them to toy buyers at $1.00—but on a non-guaranteed sale basis, which was the standard in the toy business at that time.

The publisher's best price for this $2.00 book up to that point was about $1.10, and that price had been offered only to the largest book chains. You can imagine the publisher's reaction when an unknown person from an unknown company (R&R) proposed to buy their products at less than half the price they extended to their best customers. They were prepared to reject my proposal out of hand—until I told them I would purchase all my books from them on a non-guaranteed basis.

Those were the magic words. After a brief back and forth, they agreed to my offer, which gave them a series of goodies. These included:

- **A healthy profit** at a 50-cent sales price because they had no marketing costs or commissions to pay as well as no returns.
- Access to **new channels of distribution**.

- **Economies of scale**. The cost of printing paper products like books decreases dramatically with volume. My volume, when added to their planned print runs, would reduce their cost per book and give them additional profits on all of their regular sales.

The book that they agreed to supply to me was identical in every way to the standard product, except that they printed our name (R&R) on the back cover instead of theirs. This was good for them because it clearly identified which books could not be returned. At the same time, it was good for us because it got our company name out there. Working with quality retailers like Toys "R" Us, J.C. Penney, and Sears, we sold more than 600,000 copies of the book in a short period of time, and our name was on every copy.

We also kept looking for ways to reduce our risk. For example, we asked the publisher to ship large orders direct from their factory under our label. ("Large orders" were defined as anything over 1,000 books.) In those cases we never touched the books. We also entered into a relationship with a distributor who shipped small orders, many of which we turned over to them. Everybody involved—the publisher, distributor, and retailer—was paid well for their efforts, and it was a win-win solution all around.

This venture is a good example of Bootstrapping because:

- There was zero development cost as the book was already completely developed. We just took an existing product to a new market.
- Our costs were 100% variable as we only bought a book after we sold it.
- We did not need a warehouse or shipping facility as all books were shipped from the publisher to our customers. The only charges we paid were the shipping charges, which we passed on to the customer.

- The bonus on this deal was that we had no risk since we never took the books into our inventory. Our only administrative tasks were the placing of the orders to the publisher, the billing to the customer, and the collections of invoices.

The bottom line is that outsourcing can be good and can be critical for many small companies' growth and survival. It also is a major plus if you sell a product with a short life. You can discontinue the product with no loss in equipment or molds as none were bought because of outsourcing.

19.
Government Help

GOVERNMENT HELP MAY SOUND like an oxymoron to many people. I know that I never believed any help from the government that was free was of value. I also felt the paper work that came with it was probably not worth the effort.

In exploring this avenue, I was pleasantly surprised to discover all the high quality assistance that is available to start-ups and existing Small Business that is free. In this chapter we will take a look at some of these Government entities, such as SBA, SCORE, SBDC, PTAC, Department of Commerce, U. S. Customs, U.S. Embassies, and others.

However, there seems to be one common thread with all these entities. Most small and wannabe business owners that I talk with are unaware of these agencies. If they have heard of them, they don't know how they can benefit from them.

We will highlight each entity in this chapter. Hopefully, you will be able to benefit from their free help and advice.

SBA

SBA stands for Small Business Administration. It's a large agency of the Federal government whose mission is to counsel, assist, and protect the interests of Small Business as well as to assist in the economic recovery of communities after disasters. The SBA states that they are here to help Americans start, build, and grow businesses.

The SBA is the prime source of money for SCORE, Small Business Development Centers (SBDC), Women's Business Centers (WBC), and Veterans Business Outreach Centers (VBOC). All are discussed separately.

One of the major contributions SBA makes to Small Business is their loan program. They do not loan money directly to businesses. Rather, they guarantee 75-85% of the loan that your local lender (mainly banks) will make. Applications for loans must be made to your local lender. They will ask you to fill out their forms and do their due diligence. If you fall short of their criteria, then the SBA guarantee can put you over the top for getting the loan. The maximum SBA loan is $2,000,000. In 2008, SBA approved $17.96 billion in loans at an average size of $183,000.

You should be prepared to pledge assets and sign a personal guarantee for the loan. The Small Business district offices, SCORE, and SBDC can help businesses fill out the loan application and guide you through the process. SBA will back loans for start-ups and existing Small businesses.

The SBA website: **www.sba.org** can tell you the location of the nearest office to you and detail all their services. Their phone number is 800-827-5722.

SCORE

Large companies, despite a great number of highly paid staff, hire outside consultants to advise them on a myriad of matters and pay them a great deal of money. There is a non-profit association that can act as your consultant: its point of difference is that it is free. The organization is called SCORE (formerly called Service Corps of Retired Executives) and is now referred to as "Counselors to America's Small Business."

SCORE's mission is to provide resources and expertise to maximize the success of existing and emerging small businesses.

SCORE has offices spread out over the country with 370 chapters.

They have over 11,200 volunteer executives to counsel business people who approach them for help. The business could be a start-up enterprise or an existing one.

Their service is *open to everyone* regardless of education level, race, religion, resources, etc.

SCORE was founded in 1964 and has helped millions of businesses strive for success.

SCORE counselors are uniquely qualified to help you. They have real world experience. They have specific industry and general business experience. They have a record of success in their careers. All counselors receive training in problem solving, listening, and counseling skills. They are here to provide general business advice on how to start, manage, and grow your business and are partially funded by the U.S. Small Business Administration.

Most counselors are retired, but many are still active in their own businesses. The one thing they all have in common is they are highly motivated to give back to the community by helping enterprising business people succeed. All are volunteers and have no hidden agendas.

Personally, I think they could improve in one area: the marketing of themselves. Too few know who they are.

So, I am telling you loud and clear that SCORE is there, waiting for you to call for their assistance. There is no recruiting. You have to take the first step, which is a great Bootstrapping one. All this help for FREE, NOTHING, ZIP. Got it? In this case free and quality go hand in hand.

SCORE will also provide you 24/7 help via their Internet site: **www.score.org**. There are scores of counselors with every skill available to assist you online. Your query will get an answer within 48 hours.

So, how do you get started? The first step is to find out the nearest chapter to you. This can be determined by going to their website or by calling 1-800-634-0245.

When you call your local chapter, you will be asked something about your business or would-be business. This gives them the ability to match you with the most appropriate counselor. Then you'll get an initial one-hour appointment. Most likely, the counselor will give you some homework to do before your next appointment. There are no limits to the number of appointments you can have. There can be follow up mentoring via phone and email. However, be aware, do not expect the counselor to do your work for you. They will guide you in developing a road map to success and will also point out possible pitfalls and act as the devil's advocate. Your success is dependent on your hard and smart work. Also know that SCORE does not provide money for anyone. They will, however, counsel you on all your options to raise it.

You should know that anything you tell your counselor is held in the highest confidence. All SCORE counselors sign a Code of Ethics agreement that protects and honors the privacy of the client's information.

There are no tests to pass or birthright qualifications to get an appointment. I can't see why any small business would not avail themselves of this *free*, high quality resource. I wish that I had known about SCORE when I was starting all those different businesses over my career.

SBDC

SBDC stands for Small Business Development Centers. There are nearly 1,000 centers in the United States. They are partially funded by the Federal Government through the Small Business Administration (SBA). They form a cooperative effort with the private sector, the educational community, and local government. SBA will match the amount of money contributed by the private sector and educational partner in order to operate a Small Business Center. Each year SBDC offers assistance to more than one million Small Business owners and aspiring entrepreneurs.

SBDC's mission is to provide management and technical assistance to current and prospective Small Business owners. They offer one-stop assistance to individuals and Small Businesses by providing a wide variety of information and guidance in central and easily accessible branch locations.

Their advice and counsel are *confidential and free of charge.*

There are no eligibility requirements to get their assistance. *Everyone* can use them. In 2008, 46% of SBDC business consulting clients nationwide were women, 35% were minorities, and 9% were veterans. Their counseling is on a continual basis if the entrepreneur wants it and does his/her homework.

SBDC counselors are paid employees with real business experience. SBDC regularly conducts seminars on appropriate subjects for wannabe and current business owners. They offer an extensive array of continuous courses to help you in your business and in specific industries. There are in person and online courses. Courses cover writing business plans, accessing capital, marketing, regulatory compliance, international trade, selling, customer service, accounting, and much more. These courses are offered at modest fees, and this is in addition to the free face-to-face on going counseling. The Association of Small Business Development (ASBDC), located in Burke, Virginia, states as its mission "to represent the collective interest of our members (all 1,000 SBDC Centers) by promoting, informing, supporting, and continuously improving the SBDC network which delivers nationwide educational assistance to strengthen small/medium business management, thereby contributing to the growth of local, state, and national economies. Their website is **www.asbdc-us.org**. It will give you a good understanding of SBDC and most importantly give you the location and address of the SBDC closest to you.

Each individual SBDC center has is own website. What is most interesting to me is that each individual center of the 1,000 center nation-wide network is free to adapt programs to their own environment. They are individually ENTREPRENEURIAL.

If I were to start a new business today, I would definitely avail myself of their free counseling. They are a great Bootstrapping asset.

PTAC

PTAC is a government agency funded primarily by the Department of Defense plus local government, educational institutions, and businesses. It stands for Procurement Technical Assistance Center. There are 253 centers in the country.

The PTAC's mission is to maximize the number of capable U.S. companies participating in the government marketplace,

1. providing businesses nationwide with an understanding of the requirements of government contracting and the marketing know-how they need to obtain and successfully perform federal, state, and local government contracts, and
2. supporting government agencies in reaching and working with the suppliers they need. (The government is committed to allocate a substantial amount of purchases to Small Business.)

PTACs provide a wide range of assistance—most free of charge—to businesses through one-on-one counseling, classes, seminars, and matchmaking . . . all with the goal of helping you secure contracts with all government entities including military post exchanges. They look to help all sizes companies; and there are opportunities for every type of company, whether service or product oriented. The company should be in business for at least one year. Their free of charge counselors are full time employees.

Here are some of the specific ways they can guide you through the labyrinth of procedures and regulations. Imagine, this is an agency that does more than offer counsel. They actively help you get orders with a customer who can pay their bills.

Here are some of the specific activities they perform for you:

Determining Suitability for Contracting: The government marketplace poses unique challenges that can overwhelm or even ruin a company that does not have the maturity or resources to meet them. A PTAC counselor can help you determine if your company is ready for government opportunities and how to best position yourself to succeed.

Securing Necessary Registrations: Your PTAC can help make sure you are registered with the various databases necessary for you to participate in the government marketplace, including the Department of Defense's Central Contractor Registration (CCR), the SBA's Dynamic Small Business Search, and other government vendor databases.

SDB, 8(a), HUBzone, and other certifications: Certain small businesses are eligible for preferred status in some solicitations. A PTAC counselor can help you determine if your company is eligible for any of these certifications and guide you through the steps necessary to secure them.

Researching Procurement Histories: "What agencies have bought products like yours in the past? Which companies have been awarded these contracts? How much have they been paid?" Answers to questions like these are necessary to guide your marketing strategy and give you a competitive edge. Your PTAC can help you ask the right questions and get the information you need to succeed.

Networking: Most PTACs sponsor regular "matchmaking" events, providing critical opportunities to connect with agency buying officers, prime contractors, and other businesses that may offer teaming or subcontracting opportunities.

Identifying Bid Opportunities: A PTAC can make sure that you are notified—on a daily basis—of all government contract opportunities that your company is eligible to bid on.

Proposal Preparation: A procurement specialist can help you navigate even the most difficult solicitation package, including securing necessary specifications and drawings and determining pricing. You will never need to pass up a great contract opportunity just because the solicitation is too complicated.

Contract Performance Issues: Even after you've been awarded a contract, your PTAC may be able to help with certain contract performance issues, such as

- **negotiating and interfacing with the agency**
- **developing a cost-accounting system**
- **bonding and interim financing**
- **developing environmental, quality control and accident prevention plans**

Preparing for Audit: When it's time for your contract audit, your PTAC can make sure you know what to expect and what you will need to have all documentation in order.

PTAC can also help minorities locate the special opportunities, mainly set-asides available for them.

You can go to www.aptac-us.org to locate the PTAC near you.

PTAC is a strong Bootstrapping tool.

MBDA

MBDA stands for Minority Business Development Agency. They are a part of the U.S. Department of Commerce.

The mission statement of the agency is to enhance the growth and expansion of minority business enterprise.

Their definition of minority encompasses all ethnic categories. Women are not considered a minority in this agency.

They do not loan money. Aside from advice, they seek to help Minority Small Business get government contracts.

Their website **www.wbda.gov** shows the closest office to your location. They are not in all cities.

VBOC

VBOC stands for Veterans Business Outreach Center. They have five locations in the country, each covering multiple states.

Their website: www.vboc.org will give you phone numbers, contacts, and states covered for each.

VBOC centers are designed to provide entrepreneurial development services such as business training, counseling and mentoring, plus referrals for eligible veterans owning or considering starting a Small Business.

Any former member of any branch of the US Military with an honorable discharge can seek their services free of charge. They don't loan money but can help you with counsel to raise it.

In some states, there are set-asides for disabled veterans. For those veterans who do not live near the five locations, they can be served by SBDC or SCORE.

DEPARTMENT OF COMMERCE

This is a large government agency whose head has Cabinet rank. They have offices throughout the world.

The mission of the Department is "to foster, promote, and develop the foreign and domestic commerce" of the United States.

There are many agencies under the Department of Commerce's jurisdiction. Some are Bureau of the Census, Economic Development Administration, Minority Development Agency (MBDA), U.S. Customs, and others. We talked about the MBDA. I think the Commerce Department offices in foreign countries and U.S. Customs offer specific Bootstrapping opportunities. We'll explore them here. For other information on this vast department with large amounts of information, you can visit their website: **www.commerce.gov**. Their Washington phone number is 202-482-2000.

The Commerce Department's office in Hong Kong was very helpful to me when I was in the watch business. At that time, most of the knock-offs were coming from Hong Kong. (pre-China) A number of our copyrighted watches were being copied and were showing up in the U.S. We couldn't locate the culprit. On one of my visits to Hong Kong, I dropped into the Commerce Department offices and explained my dilemma. They went out of their way to solve my problem. Through their extensive database of all manufacturers on the island, they discovered the company that was copying my watches. Knowing they had no legal authority, the Entrepreneurial Officer at the agency nevertheless wrote a firm letter on U.S. Commerce stationery to the head of the company that was manufacturing these infringed watches. That alone was enough to halt the making of these watches. My problem was solved at no cost to me. You might call this luck. However, when you think about it, one of the Commerce Department's missions is to help U.S. business in the country where they're stationed. It was obvious to me after I went there that few Americans avail themselves of this resource. Commerce would have also been a valuable asset in recommending appropriate manufacturers and providing information on the climate for conducting business there.

A number of agencies under Commerce are involved in Intellectual Property Rights in their issuance and enforcement.

There are three types of rights you can register for. I believe you can apply for two of them yourself and save legal fees by doing so.

COPYRIGHT

Copyrights protect original works of authorship such as literary, musical, sculptural, and pictorial works, motion pictures, sound recordings, computer software, and videogame software that have been fixed in a tangible medium of expression. Copyrights are registered with the United States Copyright Office.

TRADEMARKS AND TRADE NAMES

A trademark is a word, name, symbol, device, color or combination thereof used to identify and distinguish goods from those manufactured or sold by others and to indicate the source of the goods. Trademarks must be registered with the United States Patent and Trademark Office (PTO) on the Principal Register to receive IPR protection from Customs.

A trade name is the name under which a company does business. Trade names are not registered with the Patent and Trademark office, but may be recorded with Customs if the name has been used to identify a trade or manufacturer for at least six months.

PATENTS

A patent is a legal monopoly, granted by the U.S. Government, which secures to an inventor for a term of years the exclusive right to make, use, or sell his invention. The U.S. Patent and Trademark Office issues patents for novel, useful, non-obvious inventions, including processes, machines, manufactures, compositions of matter, or improvements thereof.

Custom's authority to enforce patents is much more limited than its authority to enforce trademarks and copyrights. Customs may not make legal determinations of patent infringement. Its patent enforcement authority is limited to enforcing exclusion orders issued by the U.S. International Trade Commission (ITC).

You can obtain copyrights and trademarks without needing a lawyer. Patents are more complex and hiring an Intellectual Property attorney is recommended.

The cost of a copyright is $35 if you apply online and $45 with a mailed hard copy application.

You can apply online for a copyright at **www.copyright.gov** or phone 202-707-3000 for any questions.

Trademarks cost $325 online and $375 if you apply with a hard copy through the mail.

You can apply online through the United States patent and Trademark office at www.uspto.gov. For questions, call 800-786-9199.

After you have received your copyright, trademark, or patent, you can then litigate to stop infringers. Litigation can be a costly process, and I would advise that you try to negotiate a settlement, rather than go to court. This is easier to do on copyright infringement as illustrated in our experience below.

If your protected product is copied overseas and imported to the U.S., there is a cost free way to halt these imports. Contact the U.S. Customs office and record with them your registered intellectual property. Their website is www.cbp.gov. They can then look for the infringers' shipments at our entry ports and confiscate them. This will abruptly stop the offender. However, you cannot collect damages using this route . . . but it is cost free. To collect damages, find out the U.S. users of the product and utilize a lawyer to proceed with the process of negotiating or litigating a settlement.

When we were in the watch business, we added 50+ new designs (new watches) each year. These were all original art that was done by outside freelance artists for us. We took out a copyright for each one. We did not use an attorney. Our secretary filled out each application and mailed it in to Washington, D.C., with a check for $30. Usually, within six weeks, we received our copyright approval with a unique number.

Copyrights are easy to circumvent. All you have to do is just change a portion of the art. However, most knock-off perpetrators are lazy and copy your art exactly. This happened to us quite often, and we won two suits a year. We never had to go to court. Our lawyer's letter, at a small cost, usually did the trick. If a customer was the infringer, we often settled for increased business rather than a cash settlement. Our motto became "Sell rather than Sue."

WBC's

WBC stands for Women's Business Centers. They are an agency that gets most of its funding from the SBA. They have 115 centers in the country. Their association website: **www.awbc.biz** can help you locate the center nearest you. Their mission is to help women in every phase of starting and growing a business. Their services are free of charge and are open to all women.

They can be a valuable asset to help the new entrepreneur find a female mentor. They do not loan money but can assist and counsel you on the "how to's" of raising it. Their services are similar to SBDC and SCORE with the added benefit of insights on dealing with women's issues in the workplace.

U.S. EMBASSIES

The United States has an embassy in almost every country in the world. You can go to the State Department website www.state.gov for a list of all the countries and the contacts there.

The Embassy is an out-of-the-box entity for a Small Business source. My personal story in utilizing a U.S. Embassy was when I had my watch company and acquired a license for an Elvis Pressley watch. I had noticed earlier that many retailers sold musical Mickey Mouse watches, and my research showed that these watches were made by Seiko, which owned a patent on the musical part of it. Seiko was a Japanese based company. I tried to contact them re obtaining a license or to have them make the movement for me with the Elvis tune that we would supply, and I was prepared to visit them in Japan. It was an easy stop off for me when I visited China where our watches were made. Despite numerous attempts to contact Seiko to set up an appointment, my entreaties were greeted with silence. So, as a long shot, I contacted the U.S. Embassy in Japan to ask for help in getting an appointment with Seiko. I was pleasantly surprised at their timely response in contacting management at Seiko on my behalf. This was quickly followed by my receiving a warm response from a high Seiko official, inquiring when I would like to set up an appointment to see them. When I did see them in Japan, I was ushered into an elegant conference room where 12 Seiko people were sitting, waiting to hear my story. This was an amazing outcome in my mind to a simple inquiry. A Small Business guy (although I was physically taller than everyone) all alone with 12 managers of one of the largest companies in Japan.

When you think about it, one of the missions of an Embassy is to assist American citizens visiting their country. My inquiry was a rarity and therefore got their attention. Compared to the complex problems they frequently encounter, this was an easy good deed for them to accomplish. An official request from an American Embassy can carry great weight with a foreign business in a friendly country.

The old maxim "nothing ventured, nothing gained" applies here. I believe this is as good a source to use as any to get an introduction to a firm you want to sell.

The back end to this story is after a lengthy, cordial meeting, they refused to sell me or license me their technology. They did offer to sell me their musical clocks, which I somehow believed were not good sellers for them.

Fortunately for me, six months later, someone invented a new musical watch chip, much less expensive than Seiko's, which I was able to successfully use.

LIBRARIES

The oldest source of research is still alive and well. Your local library now equipped with computers and helpful librarians as well as quiet, can be a valuable resource for your business.

They are still free. Visit them.

20.
In Perspective

THE BOOTSTRAPPING STRATEGIES IN this book can help you overcome your resources and knowledge shortcomings. This can help lead you to initial success. It takes much more for sustainable success.

Entrepreneurs are not born with special genes. Entrepreneurism is a way of thinking, which to me means it is open to anyone. I like to use the definition of Entrepreneurism by Professor Howard Stevenson, who largely invented the Entrepreneurship faculty group at Harvard Business School. His definition, with a few amendments of mine, is:

Entrepreneurship is the recognition and pursuit of opportunity without regard to the resources you currently control, with confidence that you can succeed, and the flexibility to change course as necessary, and with the will to rebound from setbacks.

This definition abounds with action words, and Successful Entrepreneurs are action oriented.

There are four major areas to concentrate on for Entrepreneurial success in my opinion. They are Attitude, Financial, People, and Knowledge. Let's examine each.

ATTITUDE

The difference between success and failure in most human endeavors can be mental . . . the attitude of the individual. Of course, knowledge, skill, and talent—and to some extent—resources are important success components. A shortfall or lack of some of these components can be overcome by one's attitude or mental makeup, which is totally controlled by the individual. This holds true in sports, business, the arts, politics, etc.

How many times have we seen the underdog player win over the more talented opponent? The difference is *attitude*.

Here are some attitude attributes to keep in mind in pursuing Entrepreneurial success.

1. **Have a passion for your business.**
   Work should be fun. Your passion will help you overcome difficult moments and persuade people to work for you and want to do business with you. *Passion* can't be taught.

2. **Set the example from Day One that you and your company are trustworthy.**
   People have confidence in trustworthy individuals and want to work for them in a culture of integrity. Ditto for customers.

3. **Be flexible except with core values.**
   It is a given that your plans and strategies must change as time goes on. This flexibility for rapid change is an inherent advantage of small over large business. However, no matter the pressure for immediate sales, do not compromise on core values.

4. **Never let up on Quality.**
   Quality is essential for *Repeat Sales*.

5. **Don't let fear of failure hold you back.**
   Failure is an opportunity to learn.

6. **Make timely decisions.**
   It's okay to use your intuition. Planning and thought are good. But procrastination will make you miss opportunities.

7. **The major company asset is you.**
   Take care of yourself. Maintain your energy level. Your health is more valuable than the most expensive machinery or computer software for the company.

8. **Keep your ego under control.**
   Don't take newfound profits and spend them on expensive toys to impress others. Build a war chest for unexpected needs or opportunities.

9. **New product ideas need not be blockbusters.**
   This also holds for starting a new company. It's hard to reinvent the wheel. It's a little like Scrabble. Add one letter to an existing word and get full credit for the entire word. Build on an existing product or service but do it better, add value, sell to a new market, build a license around it, etc.

10. **Maintain balance.**
    It doesn't have to be your family or your company. Play or work, etc.
    This will enhance your mental outlook, which is what we're talking about.

11. **Encourage and accept criticism graciously. Admit your mistakes.**
    You need to constantly work on convincing your employees that it's okay even necessary to state their honest opinions even it if conflicts with the boss. Just stating it once or putting it in a mission statement won't cut it for most people.

12. **Create an environment where innovation can flourish.**
    This means hearing out new ideas and suggestions no matter how crazy they sound.

13. Maintain a strong work ethic.

Your employees will follow your lead. It will also help you beat your competition by outworking them . . . particularly when your product or service is very similar.

14. Rebound quickly from setbacks.

There surely will be plenty of ups and downs as you build the business. Learn from the setbacks and move on. You can't change the past.

15. Periodically get out of your comfort zone to pursue something important.

Many times you will feel uncomfortable in implementing a needed change in technology, people, mission, competing, etc. For the company and you to grow personally, you sometimes have to step out of your comfort zone.

FINANCIAL

One of the most essential skills that you can personally bring to your company is understanding, tracking, and using certain numbers. You don't need an accountant for this. Simple math and focus are required. You want to get to the point where you think in numbers. I like to call this numeracy. Early stage companies can't afford full-time comptrollers. Even when you can and have a competent accountant, the person running the company should always be aware of the numbers. Let's look at these financial points.

1. Always watch the cash.

The number one reason for companies failing is running out of cash. You need to always know your cash position, when new cash is coming in, and when bills need to be paid. What you need is a *Cash Flow* statement. This should be done on a monthly basis. In high peak seasons, maybe more often. The statement looks a little different depending on your industry. A service business does not have to take inventory into account like a product business does. The bottom line is you need to be sure you will have cash on hand to pay bills as they come due. Profits don't necessarily mean cash availability. You can get help in learning how to prepare a cash flow statement for your business from an accountant, your local SCORE or SBDC office, books, or the Internet. Incidentally, a cash flow statement is a must if you want to borrow money. It will indicate when you can pay back the loan. In Appendix 3, I have put forth an outline on how you can create a Cash Flow statement and an example of one.

2. **Don't forget the details. Be diligent in monitoring your numbers.**

To capture all the key details and numbers, I use what I call a Company Snapshot. I prefer to see it weekly. You can vary the interval based on your liquidity, seasonality, and special factors of your business. You also can change some of the components you are tracking, based on your business and needs. (See example.)

Here is what the **Company Snapshot** looks like.

Current assets
  Cash   _____
  Cash equivalent   _____
  Receivables   _____
  Other   _____

    TOTAL   _____

Inventory
  Finished   _____
  Component   _____

    TOTAL   _____

Current liabilities
  Payables   _____
    Misc.   _____
  Accrued commissions   _____
  Accrued royalties   _____

    TOTAL   _____

Fixed monthly expenses   _____
Loans outstanding   _____
Monthly sales to date   _____
Yearly sales to date   _____
Future orders to ship   _____
Purchase orders   _____

This snapshot should be adjusted for your special needs. A service company would take out the Inventory component. If you have no licenses or sales reps, then the commission and royalty lines can be omitted.

The receptionist or secretary can learn to fill this out for you, but you have to read and understand it. After a while, it will take five minutes of your time to digest it. Potential problems will jump out at you. For instance, higher than normal receivables without corresponding sales increases could mean your customer collection person is operating on a sub par level or one of your customers is in deep trouble.

3. **Profits are good and essential.**
    Don't be embarrassed by them.
    Many in the media and academia frown on business and their greedy profiteers. Pay them no heed. They are in the minority; but most importantly, without a business making a profit, it is not sustainable. This is particularly true of small business as capital is much less available to them than the large corporations that can sustain losses for long periods. So always keep your eye on the profits, and remember that most of the job creation in the country comes from small business.

4. **Always pay your bills on time.**
    This was discussed at length in the Suppliers chapter. It should be a cardinal rule in the company as the benefits of doing so can be enormous. This is one of the major reasons you are doing cash flow statements: to make sure you can pay on time.

5. **Convert Fixed Costs to Variable where feasible.**
    This is covered in Chapter 3. Doing so can affect your finances in a major way. It reduces your financial risks and lowers your cash needs in slow times.

6. **The break-even analysis.**
    This is a tool that is sometimes overlooked, even though it is easy to determine and gives you valuable information in a

number of different contexts. The break-even tells you in dollars or units what amount of sales you need to achieve in order to recoup all your fixed costs or investment. Are you trying to decide whether to proceed with a new product introduction? Are you trying to understand exactly where costs stop and start for your company? Are you trying to decide whether to buy a company? In all of these cases, the break-even analysis should be your tool of choice.

To do a break-even on a *product:*

    a. Determine the cost of the product (let's say it's $9).
    b. Determine the average selling price ($20).
    c.. Subtract **a** from **b**, which gives you your profit contribution per unit ($11).
    d. Determine the total investment required for that product ($80,000).
    e. Divide **c** into **d**. The result is the break-even (in this case 7,273 units).

Once you know the break-even for a given product, you can ask the critical questions. Is it reasonable to attain the break-even sales figure based on (1) the offering, and (2) our knowledge of the current market? In light of the resources that will be required to bring this product to market, how risky is this bet?

A good example of doing a break-even analysis is in Appendix 1, the R&R TV Guide case. The game/toy business is a high-risk product business, particularly with a fad item in a one-product business with a new company. However, with a break-even of 11,709 units and 5 free full-page ads worth $425,000, all risk disappears. One customer that received an ad placed an opening order more than 3 times the break-even.

7. **Don't be afraid to give up equity under the right circumstances.**

    In some cultures, the business owner is paranoid about giving up equity no matter the circumstance. There are times when selling equity in your enterprise is your only or best option. This is particularly true when the investor brings more to your table than money. It's the old story: would you rather own 100% of a company that yields $100,000 profit a year or 60% of a company with $1,000,000 a year in profits?

PEOPLE

There is a lot of truth in the adage that a company is as good as the people working in it. Hiring quality people is a challenge for a start-up or existing small business. Usually because of your cash crunch, you can't pay competitive salaries. The company probably has not proven its sustainability yet. The founder may be inexperienced. The company benefits don't match corporate America's, etc. So how do you get quality people to work for you? Your passion and vision can be a great recruiting tool. They need to feel good about your integrity and believe they will be treated fairly and rewarded if they perform and the company prospers. As you grow and are successful and want to either go public or sell your company, be aware that the Venture Capitalists or acquiring company will give high credence to the quality of your employees. If they are sub par or show low motivation, it will reflect poorly on you as a leader.

Here are some of the people issues you should address:

1. **Look to hire people different than yourself (can be smarter) who speak up and are curious. Incentivize them. Give them a sense of inclusion.**

    Don't make the mistake of only hiring people who look like you and share your interests. You want bright people. If they are smarter than you, then the company will benefit and so will you.

These are the people that will be at the forefront of your innovation initiatives.

2. **Don't try to do everything yourself. Delegate but with the authority that goes with it.**

You may know every facet of your business better than all of your employees. However, to grow, you can't do it all yourself. For many company founders, it is very difficult to give up some of their duties. Those that resist discover the hard way that they must do so to personally survive and for the business to move ahead. Where you do delegate, you must give the person responsible the authority to get the job done. Let them make some mistakes. It will allow them to grow and be a more educated and reliable employee.

3. **Credit employees' successes. Tell them your expectations of them.**

If you are going to criticize poor performance, then praise success. If you want your people to be responsible and grow, lay out in clear language what you expect of them. People appreciate knowing the rules of the game. They are more highly motivated when they do.

4. **Promote teamwork, punish internal politics.**

Your business is like a team. There is no "i" in team. Healthy egos are good as long as they further the team (company) goals and don't undermine fellow workers. Human behavior being what it is, unhealthy politics seem to creep into the culture, particularly when the roster increases. You have to let it be clearly known that mutual respect and civility must prevail in your company. It will aid the motivation and innovation of all.

5. **Make sure customers' expectations are met. Under commit and over perform.**

The "Customer is King" must continually be reinforced. Pressure to meet quotas must not result in false customer promises to garner a quick sale. You always want happy customers and your people should be motivated to go the extra mile for them. Customers are people.

6. **Treat good suppliers like gold.**
   The chapter on suppliers spells out all the reasons why suppliers can affect the good health of your company. If you are the person who deals face to face with the supplier and another company department is acting in a way to hurt the relationship, you must take action. Don't stand idly by and then blame someone else when the relationship deteriorates. A good example is if your finance department is not paying the bills on time, find out why and if it's not a good reason, let them or your boss know it is not acceptable.

7. **You are judged by the company you keep. Align with quality partners.**
   This can mean licensors, top grade customers, your accountant, lawyer, marketing partners, etc. Your would-be customers may not know you well but know and respect your partners.

8. **Move quickly to fire people you are convinced are bad for your company.**
   When I interviewed the 27 entrepreneurs for my first book, I asked them all what actions they took in business that they regretted? The almost unanimous answer was they waited too long to fire the bad apples in the company. For most people, firing is an unpleasant task that brings on procrastination. First, everyone in the company usually knows the poor performing person. If they are left to continue in the company, then it affects all employees as they begin to question why should they work so hard when that goof-off doesn't, and we both get the

same rewards. Before firing, I would put the person on notice that he/she is not performing to the company's expectations and tell them in writing what they need to improve. Maybe additional training is required. If there is no improvement, you must fire the person. A bad employee contaminates the entire workplace.

9. **As the company grows, people's roles change, including yours. Can you/they adapt, and what will you do with people who can't? This includes partners.**
    Continued success breeds new challenges. This is one of them. At the outset of the company, the few employees do many functions, including each other's. As it grows, people need to adapt to special roles, which they may not have the skill or knowledge to do well. New employees can be resented by the old guard. The company's mission, emphasis, goals, and chemistry can change. Some people who were good workers can't adapt to these changes. These kinds of people problems can be difficult to resolve. You, however, should look for them and when they appear, deal with them early on.

KNOWLEDGE

Knowledge truly is power. It lets you recognize opportunity and helps you pursue it. The more knowledge you possess about your industry, business in general, people, the environment, etc., the greater your chances of success. Knowledge and its growth apply to your employees also. Here are some knowledge thoughts to keep in mind.

1. **Know what you don't know.**
    Learning is much easier when you know what to learn. Also, in most cases your credibility is enhanced if you say, "I don't know." For many, it is not easy to do.

2. **Know your business: product, industry, and competition. Knowledge rules.**
   Self-explanatory.

3. **Work on your listening as well as your communication skills.**
   Good listening is a skill that can be learned. You are already equipped with the ability to hear, a starting point. There are books and videos on the subject. I believe you truly have to want to listen. If you do, people will trust you more, you'll learn more, and be a much more effective communicator which includes selling.

4. **Work on your sales skills and everyone else's in your company.**
   Everyone should sell (as explored in the selling chapter). Persuasion is enhanced by knowledge of the person you are trying to sell, his/her company, goals, environment, motivations, etc. It is a learnable skill.

5. **Plan for tomorrow. In planning your strategies, ask why should your prospective customer buy from you?**
   Again your knowledge of the customer and the full ramifications and resources needed for your strategy will help ensure the success of your planning.

6. **Look for mentors and work hard at building the relationship.**
   The chapter on mentors explains how a mentor expedites your learning process and reduces the risk factor in the business.

7. **Working smart is as important as working hard.**
   In times past, outworking your competition usually insured success. It still works to a certain extent. However, there is more

and generally smarter competition today. You, therefore, need to work smart.

8. **Keep learning.**

   This is a lifetime mantra which should be part of your DNA. Think doctors. They must always enhance their knowledge of new medical breakthroughs and medicines. The obsolescence of their medical school learning is high. Their work is more life and death. Although if you stop learning, it could eventually be the death of your company.

RISK

We have not specifically focused on risk per se. Contrary to the portrayal of Entrepreneurs in the media, they don't love to take risks. I've never met one that jumped out of bed on a beautiful day and said, "Where can I find risk today?" They carefully measure it, try to avoid it as much as possible, share it, stage it, reduce it, and then face it if the risk/reward ratio looks good. However, most of the Bootstrap tips offered here reduce risk. Costs that are variable, outsourcing, correct pricing, better selling, free ads, good suppliers, licensing and free quality advice are all risk reducers.

FINAL THOUGHT

Don't be intimidated about all the factors you have to deal with to run a successful business. You don't have to excel at all of them. Try to keep some of the most important ones in the forefront. Maintain your passion, watch the cash, treat people with respect, keep learning, and most of all, don't forget that the name of the game is acquire customers and keep them satisfied. They will reward you with continuous business and give you the best advertising in the world at no charge: GOOD WORD OF MOUTH.

APPENDICES

Appendix 1.
R & R Case Study

THE R&R CASE:

The case that follows and has been discussed in the introduction has been taught at the Harvard Business School and the Columbia Business School for the past 20 years. I know this for a fact because I've attended almost all of these case discussions.

I'm told that the case also has been taught at more than fifty other business schools around the United States at the undergraduate, graduate, and executive-program levels. I have personally spoken to classes discussing R&R at the following schools: Harvard, Columbia, Miami University of Ohio, Northwestern University, UCLA, Babson College, Arizona State University, George Washington University, Boston University, The University of Wisconsin, Florida Atlantic University, Monmouth University, and Fairleigh Dickinson University. The case is shown here in its entirety as written by Harvard Business School. It is followed by my comments on how the Bootstrap tips that have been put forth in this book were employed. I'd like to thank the Harvard Business School and Howard Stevenson for writing this case and for giving me permission to reprint it in this context.

Harvard Business School Case 386-019. Reprinted by permission of Harvard Business School.

During the summer of 1983, Bob Reiss observed with interest the success in the Canadian market of a new board game called "Trivial Pursuit." His years of experience selling games in the U.S. had taught him a rough rule of thumb: the sales of a game in the U.S. tended to be approximately ten times those of sales in Canada. Since "Trivial Pursuit" had sold 100,000 copies north of the border, Reiss thought that trivia games might soon boom in the U.S., and that this might represent a profitable opportunity for him.

<u>Reiss' Background</u>

After his graduation from Harvard Business School in 1956, Reiss began working for a company that made stationery products. His main responsibility was to build a personalized pencil division, and he suggested that he be paid a low salary and a high sales commission. He was able to gain an excellent understanding of that market, and by 1959 could start on his own as an independent manufacturer's representative in the same industry. His direct contact with stores that sold stationery products revealed that many of them were beginning to sell adult games. He decided to specialize in those products.

In 1973, Reiss sold his representative business to a small American Stock Exchange company in the needlecraft business in exchange for shares. He then set up a game manufacturing division and ran it for that company, building sales to $12,000,000 in three years.

Reiss decided to go into business for himself again in 1979 and left the company. He incorporated under the name of R&R and worked with the help of a secretary from a rented office in New York; Reiss promised himself that he would keep overhead very low, even in good years, and never own or be responsible for a factory. In addition to being a traditional manufacturer's representative, he did some consulting for toy manufacturers, using his extensive knowledge of the market.

This case was prepared by Research Assistant Jose-Carlos Jarillo Mossi, under the supervision of Professor Howard H. Stevenson, as the basis for class discussion rather than to illustrate either effective or ineffective handling of an administrative situation.

The Toy and Game Industry

One of the main characteristics of the toy industry was that products generally had very short life cycles, frequently of no more than two years. "Fads" extended to whole categories of items: one class of toys would sell well for a couple of years and then fade away. Products that were part of categories tended to ride with the fate of that category, regardless to some extent of their intrinsic merit. Many new products were introduced every year, which made the fight for shelf space aggressive.

Promotional plans for a new product were a key factor in buy or no-buy decisions of the major retailers. At the same time, fewer and fewer retailers were dominating more of the market every year. The largest one, Toys 'R' Us, for example, had 14% of the entire market in 1984. The success of a product was often based on less than a dozen retailers.

A few large manufacturers were also becoming dominant in the industry, because they could afford the expensive TV promotional campaigns that retailers demanded of the products they purchased. Billing terms to retailers were extremely generous compared to other industries, thus increasing the need for financial strength. Financing terms ran from a low of 90 days to 9 to 12 months. In general, major retailers were reluctant to buy from new vendors with narrow product lines unless they felt that the volume potential was enormous. On the other hand, the large manufacturers tended to require a long lead time for introducing new products, typically on the order of 18 to 24 months.

The industry was also highly seasonal. Most final sales to the public were made in the four weeks prior to Christmas. Retailers decided what to carry for the Christmas season during the preceding January through March. There was a growing tendency among them, however, not to accept delivery until the goods were needed, in effect using the manufacturer as their warehouse.

The Trivia Game Opportunity

"Trivial Pursuit" was developed in Canada, and introduced there in 1980. Its 1983 sales were exceptionally strong, especially for a product that had been promoted primarily via word of mouth. The game was introduced in the U.S. at the Toy Fair in February, 1983 by Selchow & Righter, makers of "Scrabble," under license from Horn & Abbot in Canada. Earlier, the game had been turned down by Parker Bros. and Bradley, the two largest game manufacturers in the United States.

"Trivial Pursuit" in the U.S. had a $19.00 wholesale price, with a retail price varying from $29.95 to $39.95, about 200% to 300% more expensive than comparable board games. Selchow was not known as a strong marketer and had no TV advertising or public relations budget for the game. The initial reaction at the Toy Fair in February had been poor. Yet, by August the game had started moving at retail.

Reiss thought that if the success of "Trivial Pursuit" in Canada spilled over to the U.S., the large game companies would eventually produce and market their own similar products. This would generate popular interest in trivia games in general and constitute a window of opportunity for him. The only trivia game in the market as of September 1983 was "Trivial Pursuit." Two small firms had announced their entries and were taking orders for the next season. Bob Reiss decided to design and market his own trivia game.

Developing the Concept

Reiss' first task was to find an interesting theme, one that would appeal to as broad an audience as possible. On one hand, he wanted to capitalize on the new "trivia" category that "Trivial Pursuit" would create; on the other, he wanted to be different, and therefore could not use a topic already covered by that game, such as movies or sports. Further, his game would have its own rules, yet be playable on the "Trivial Pursuit" board.

As was his custom, Reiss discussed these ideas with some of his closest friends in the manufacturer's representative business. Over the years, he had found them a source of good ides. One of the reps suggested television as a topic. Reiss saw immediately that this had great potential: not only did it have a broad appeal (the average American family watches over seven hours of TV per day), it offered a great PR opportunity. A strong PR campaign would be needed since Reiss knew clearly that he was not going to be able to even approach the advertising budgets of the large manufacturers, which would probably surpass $1 million just for their own trivia games.

Because licensing was common in the toy industry and was a way to obtain both an easily recognizable name and a partner who could help promote the product, Reiss realized he could add strength and interest to his project if he could team up with the publishers of TV Guide. This magazine had the highest diffusion in the U.S., approaching 18 million copies sold each week. It reached more homes than any other publication and could be called a household name.

On October 17, 1983, Reiss sent a letter, printed below, to Mr. Eric Larson, publisher of T.V. Guide.

Mr. Eric Larson, Publisher   October 17, 1983
T.V. GUIDE
P.O. Box 500
Radnor, PA 19088

Dear Mr. Larson:

I am a consultant in the game industry and former owner of a game
company.

Briefly, I would like to talk to you about creating a game and
marketing plan for a 'T.V. GUIDE TRIVIA GAME'.

In 1984, trivia games will be a major classification of the Toy
Industry. I'm enclosing copy of a forthcoming ad that will
introduce a game based upon the 60 years of Time Magazine. I am
the marketer of this game and have received a tremendous response
to the game, both in orders and future publicity.

This project can benefit both of us, and I would like to explore
the opportunities.

                                        Sincerely,

                                        Robert S. Reiss

        In a follow-up phone conversation, Mr. Bill Deitch, assistant to
the publisher of the magazine, asked Reiss for some detailed explanation on
the idea. Reiss sent the following proposal:

Mr. Bill Deitch   November 14, 1983
T.V. GUIDE
P.O. Box 500
Radnor, PA 19088

Dear Mr. Deitch:

In response to our phone conversation, I will attempt to briefly
outline a proposal to do a TV Trivia Game by TV Guide.

WHY A TV GAME? It is a natural follow up to the emerging craze
of Trivia Games that is sweeping the country. This category
should be one of the 'Hot' categories in the Toy/Game industry in
1984. This type of game got its start in Canada three years ago
with the introduction of Trivial Pursuit. It continues to be the
rage in Canada and was licensed in the U.S. this year. It is
currently the top selling non-electronic game. It retails from
$24.95 to $39.95 and is projected to sell 1,000,000 units. It is

not TV promoted. The 'Time Game', with 8,000 questions covering six general subject areas, only began to ship two weeks ago and had an unprecedented initial trade buy, particularly with no finished sample available for prior inspection.

WILL TV GUIDE BE JUST ANOTHER TRIVIA GAME? No. The next step is to do specialty subjects. Trivial Pursuit has just done a Motion Picture Game with excellent success. Our research tells us that a TV oriented game would have the broadest national appeal.

THE MARKETS - This type of game has wide appeal in that it is non-sexual and is of interest to adults and children. We feel we can place it in over 10,000 retail outlets ranging from upscale retailers like Bloomingdale's and Macy's to mass merchants like Toys 'R' Us, Sears, Penney, K-Mart, Target, etc. There is also a good mail-order market. The market is particularly receptive to good playing, social interactive games at this time. Video games are in a state of decline as their novelty has worn off. (To say nothing about profits).

WHO WILL DEVELOP THE GAME? Alan Charles, a professional game developer who did the 'Time Game', is free at this moment to do work on the project. He has satisfied the strict standards 'Time' has set for putting its name on a product and mine for play value and product graphics in a highly competitive market... No easy task.

WHO WILL PRODUCE & MARKET THE GAME? There are two options for producing the game.

1. Give it to an established game company who would assume all financial risk as well as production and distribution responsibilities. Under this set-up, TV Guide would get a royalty on all goods sold.

2. TV Guide assume all financial responsibilities to game. Production and shipping would be handled by a contract manufacturer. Bob Reiss would be responsible for hiring and supervising a national sales force to sell the game. This is not an unusual option, and I do have experience in this. All sales are on a commission basis. This way, TV Guide gets the major share of the profits.

    Attached exhibit explores some rough profit numbers for TV Guide, via both options.

POSITIONING OF GAME - We see the game as non-competitive to Trivial Pursuit and Time Magazine. It can be developed to retail at $14.95, as opposed to $39.95 for Trivial Pursuit and $29.95 for Time. (Mass merchants generally discount from these list prices). The TV Game should be able to be played by owners of both games as well as on its own. The name 'TV Guide' is important to the credibility of the product. Sales of licensed products have been growing at geometric rates in the last decade.

Consumers are more comfortable buying a product with a good name
behind it.

PROMOTION OF GAME - Pricing of the product will have an ad
allowance built into it. This will allow the retailers to
advertise in their own catalog, tabloids and/or newspaper ads.
An important part of promotion should be ads in TV Guide. Ads
can be handled two ways: one, with mail order coupon and profits
accruing to TV Guide; the other, with listing of retailers
carrying the item, as you have so many regional splits, the
listing could be rather extensive. Financially, you would
probably opt for the first option on a royalty arrangement and
the second if you owned the product.

This product lends itself perfectly to an extensive public
relations program. This is an excellent product for radio
stations to promote. This should be pursued vigorously.

BENEFITS TO TV GUIDE

... Profits from royalties or manufacturing
... Extensive publicity through wide distribution on U.S. retail
    counter, including the prestigious retailers as well as the
    volume ones. This is the unique type of product that can
    bridge this gap.
... Good premium for your clients. Can be excellent premium for
    TV Stations. Can be used as a circulation builder. In
    projecting profits, I have not included premiums. The
    numbers can be big, but they are difficult to count on.

TIMING To effectively do business in 1984, all contracts must be
done and a prototype developed for the American Toy Fair, which
takes place in early February, 1984. Shipments need not be made
until late spring.

WHO IS BOB REISS? He is a graduate of Columbia College and
Harvard Business School who started his own national rep firm in
1959, specializing in adult games, when it became a distinct
category in 1968. He sold his company in 1973 to an American
Stock Exchange Company. He remained there for five years and
built Reiss Games to a dominant position in the adult-game field.
For the last three years, he has been consulting in the game/toy
industry and recently acted as broker in the sale of one of his
clients, Pente Games, to Parker Bros.

I am enclosing some articles that have a bearing on the subject
matter. I think what is needed, as soon as possible, is a face-
to-face meeting, where we can discuss in greater detail all
aspects of this proposal as well as responsibilities for all
parties.

                                    Sincerely,
RSR/ck   Robert S. Reiss
encl.

ROUGH PROFIT POTENTIALS TO TV GUIDE

ASSUMPTIONS

1. Average wholesale cost of $7.15 after all allowances. (This would allow Department Stores and Mail Order to sell at $15.00 Discounters would sell at $9.95 to $11.95).

2. Cost to manufacture, $3.00 each.

3. Royalty rate of 10% - (Range is 6% to 10%, depending on licensor support and name. Assuming 10%, based on fact you would run No Cost ads in TV Guide).

4. Mail order retail in TV Guide is $14.95, and you would pay $4.00 for goods. Postage and Handling would be a wash with small fee charged to customer.

OPTION I - ROYALTY BASIS

Projected Retail Sales - 500,000 units.
     *Royalty to TV Guide of $357,500

Mail Order Sales - 34,000 units (.002 pull on 17,000,000 circulation). Based on full-page ad with coupon. It is extremely difficult to project mail order sales without testing-- too many variables. However, this is a product that is ideal for your audience.
     * Profit to TV Guide of $372,300

OPTION II - YOU OWN GOODS

Costs: (Rough Estimate)

Manufacture	$3.00
Royalties to inventor	.36
Fulfillment	.30
Sales Costs	1.43
Amortization of start-up costs	.10
TOTAL COST	$5.19
Profit per unit	$1.96

Profit on 500,000 units = $980,000.00
(Does not include cost of money.)

Another phone conversation followed in which TV Guide showed a clear interest in pursuing the subject. Reiss answered with a new letter on December 12, 1983, that outlined clearly the steps that had to be followed by both parties should they want to go ahead with the venture. Reiss had to send still another letter with a long list of personal references that TV Guide could contact. TV Guide finally opted to be a licensor, not a manufacturer. They would give Bob Reiss a contract for him to manufacture the game or farm it out to an established manufacturer, provided he stayed involved with the project. TV Guide would receive a royalty that would escalate with volume. Royalties were normally paid quarterly, over shipments; Reiss, however, proposed to pay over money collected, which TV Guide accepted. As part of the final deal, TV Guide would insert, at no cost, five ads in the magazine worth $85,000 each. These would be "cooperative ads"; that is, the name of the stores selling the game in the area of each edition would also be displayed. Reiss thought that including the name of the stores at no cost to them would be a good sales argument and would help insure a wide placement of the product.

Developing the TV Guide Trivia Game

The actual game was designed by a professional inventor, whom Reiss knew, in exchange for a royalty of 5%--decreasing to 3% with volume--per game sold. No up-front monies were paid or royalties guaranteed. Although the inventor delivered the package design in just a few weeks, the questions to be asked were not yet formulated, and Reiss realized he could not do this alone. TV Guide's management insisted that their employees should develop them. Reiss would pay per question for each of the 6,000 questions he needed; employees could moonlight on nights and weekends. Reiss felt it was important to put questions and answers in books rather than cards, like "Trivial Pursuit." The cost would be considerably lower, and the most serious bottleneck in manufacturing-- collating the cards--would be eliminated. The game also lent itself well to this approach, as the question books imitated the appearance of TV Guide magazine (Exhibit 1). Overall, the presentation of the game tried to capitalize on the well-known TV Guide name (Exhibit 2).

Initially, Reiss had not wanted to include a board with the game; he wanted people to use "Trivial Pursuit's" board and had made sure that the rules of the new game would take this into account. However, TV Guide wanted a complete game of its own, not just supplementary questions to be played on someone else's game. Another advantage of including a board, Reiss realized, was that a higher price could be charged.

Since TV Guide had opted for being merely a licensor, it was Reiss' responsibility to set up all the operations needed to take the game to market in time for the 1984 season, and there were only two months left until the February Toy Fair, where the game had to be introduced.

His first consideration was financial. He estimated that the fixed cost of developing the product would be between $30,000 and $50,000, but some $300,000 would be needed to finance the first production run. Those funds would be needed until the initial payments from sales arrived a few months later.

Reiss seriously considered raising the required money from the strongest among his manufacturer's representatives in the toy business, thinking they would push hard to sell the game to every account. Eventually, he decided against this approach: not only would it not contribute that much to the venture, reps could be motivated to sell in other ways. Perhaps more important, Reiss feared the prospect of perhaps 20 partners who "would be every day on the phone asking how things are going."

Another option that passed through his mind, which he dismissed promptly, was venture capital. He realized that he would have to give up too much and, even worse, that venture capitalists would not understand this kind of deal--one that had very attractive short-term profits but few long-term prospects.

Trivia, Inc.

With the agreement with TV Guide in hand, Reiss called Sam Kaplan--a long-time friend who lived in Chicago. Kaplan, 65 years old, had a sizeable personal net worth, yet kept working at his small but successful advertising agency (25 employees) "for the fun of it," as he liked to say. Reiss thought that teaming up could be an important help, and Kaplan was indeed enthusiastic about the idea.

Reiss proposed to establish a company, Trivia Inc., that would develop the project. The equity would be split evenly among the two partners. Kaplan, besides lending his line of credit to purchase supplies for the initial run, would use his office to handle day-to-day details. (In fact, Trivia Inc. ended up having only one full-time employee.) Also, because of his vast knowledge of printing and his contacts, Kaplan could secure press time and paper supplies on short notice, and he would supervise the product's manufacturing. This was especially important, since the special paper stock on which the game was printed was then in short supply, and long lead times were generally needed to obtain it. Kaplan would also produce all the ads and the catalog sheets. Reiss would take responsibility for sales and marketing of the product and would pay all reps and coordinate the publicity and the relations with TV Guide. An important part of the agreement was that R&R (Reiss' company) would have the exclusive rights to market the game and would receive a commission of 20% of the wholesale price from which it would pay the commissions to the reps.

Production, Shipping and Billing

From the beginning, Reiss' intention was not to be a manufacturer. Through Kaplan's connections, they found not only good suppliers for the question books, the board and the boxes, they even got lower costs than expected. But, they still had to tackle the problem of assembly and shipping. Kaplan was a long-time consultant to Swiss Colony, a manufacturer of cheese based in Madison, Wisconsin. This company specialized in mail sales and had developed a strong capability to process mail orders. As a result, Swiss Colony's management had decided several years earlier to offer that fulfillment capability to other companies. They took the orders, shipped the product, and billed to the retailer.

In the deal ultimately reached, Trivia Inc. would have the components sent by the different suppliers to Madison on a "just in time" basis, and Swiss Colony would put the boards, dice, and questions in the boxes, package and ship them. Swiss Colony would charge $.25 per box, including billing for the games, and would send complete daily information on sales to Trivia Inc. Trivia Inc. would pay $2,500 for a customized computer program. With all these measures, Reiss and Kaplan were able to lower their estimated costs by 30% and attained the flexibility they wanted. The final cost of manufacturing, assembling and shipping was about $3.10, not including the royalties paid to the inventor and to TV Guide.

A final point was financing the accounts receivable, once the sales started rolling in, and collecting the debts. Reiss was somewhat afraid that the bills of some of the smaller stores carrying the game would be very difficult to collect, since R&R did not have the resources to follow-up closely on its collections; moreover, Trivia Inc. needed the leverage of a factor in order to collect from the larger retailers on time. He and Kaplan decided to use Heller Factoring to check credit, guarantee payment, collect the money, and pay Trivia Inc., all for a fee of 1% over sales. Trivia Inc. would not need any financing for operations: after 45 days of shipping, Trivia Inc. would always be in a positive cash-flow. Thanks to Heller and Swiss Colony, Trivia Inc. had practically no administrative work left to itself.

Selling the Game

Selling was the most important issue for Reiss. He knew that placing the goods in the stores and selling them to the public (selling through) were two distinct, many times unrelated, problems. In any case, however, he thought that the game needed to be priced below "Trivial Pursuit" to make up for both their lack of a complete national advertising campaign that major manufacturers would launch, and their lack of the kind of brand recognition that "Trivial Pursuit" was achieving. Accordingly, the wholesale price was set at $12.50, with a retail list price of $25.

Reiss distinguished carefully between two different channels: the mass merchandisers and the department/gift stores. An important part of the overall strategy was to sell quickly to upscale retailers who would establish a full retail mark-up (50%). These were mainly department stores, such as Bloomingdale's or Marshall Fields, and mail order gift catalogs and specialty gift stores. This, it was hoped, would help sell mass merchandisers and give them a price from which to discount. Such a two-tiered approach was not common in the industry. On long-life products, many times only the full-margin retailers got the product the first year. But Reiss felt that this could not be done with his product, because it could well be only a one-year product. Mass merchandisers, however, had to be reached, since they accounted for at least 75% of the market. (Exhibit 3 shows some of the stores Reiss thought had to be reached.)

Two different sets of reps were employed for the two different channels; on average, they received a 7% commission on sales. Reiss' personal knowledge of buyers for the major chains proved invaluable. He was able to obtain quick access to the important decision-makers at the major chains. They also followed, when possible, the distribution pattern of TV Guide magazine. It was soon apparent that the statistics on demographics reached by TV Guide, which Reiss made sure all buyers saw

(Exhibit 4), had a major impact. As Reiss said, "It appeared that every
outlet's customers read TV Guide." The cooperative ads in the magazine,
with the possibility of including the store's name, were also a powerful
attraction for different buyers, as Reiss had expected: the name of their
stores would be displayed in far more homes that it would with a
conventional advertising campaign in national magazines. The stores would
not be charged to have their name in the ads, but minimum purchase orders
would be requested. Many large customers, such as K-Mart and Sears, placed
large orders before the product was even finished. (Exhibit 5 shows a
cover letter that was sent to supermarket buyers.)

Promotion

        In order to promote the game to the public, Trivia Inc. had a
four-part plan, beginning with the five ads in TV Guide. (Exhibit 6) The
first ad broke in mid-September, 1984, and was strictly for upscale
retailers, with $25.00 as the price of the game. TV Guide had eight
regional issues, and different stores were listed in each area with a total
of about 120, including Bloomingdale's, Marshall Fields, Jordan Marsh and
J.C. Penney. They all had to place minimum orders. The second ad, shown
on October 6th, was just for Sears. The third, on November 10th, was
devoted to mass merchandisers and did not include a retail price. The
fourth, two weeks later, listed four of the most important toy chains: Toys
'R' Us, Child World, Lionel Leisure and Kay Bee. The appeal to the public,
then, was not just the ad: Reiss knew that showing well-known upscale
stores carrying the game initially was the best way to obtain instant
credibility for the product. Finally, K-Mart, the largest U.S. Chain, gave
Trivia Inc. an opening order to all their 2,100 stores, even before the
game went into production, in exchange for the exclusivity in the fifth ad
to be run in TV Guide on December 8, 1984. In that ad, K-Mart offered a
three-day sale at $16.97.

        The second part of the plan also tried to give credibility to the
game. Trivia Inc. offered the department stores a 5% ad allowance (a 5%
discount from wholesale price) if they put the product in newspaper ads,
tabloids or catalogs. For similar reasons, Reiss wanted to have the game
placed in mail order gift catalogs. Their sales in the toy-game business
were only moderate, but catalogs gave a lot of product exposure because of
their large circulation figures.

        The final part of the plan was to obtain free media publicity.
The publisher of TV Guide magazine wrote a letter to be sent to the
producers of such shows as "Good Morning, America," "CBS Morning News,"
"The Tonight Show," and to 25 top TV personalities, together with a sample
of the game. Through TV Guide's P.R. agency and the joint efforts of TV
Guide and Trivia Inc., many newspapers, radio and TV stations were reached.
In all, more than 900 press kits were sent to media organizations. As a
result, the game was mentioned on many talk shows (TV and radio), and news
of it was published in many newspapers (Exhibit 7). The cost of this
campaign was split between Trivia Inc. and TV Guide.

The Results

By October 1983, Selchow, manufacturer of "Trivial Pursuit," started falling behind trying to meet the demand. By Christmas, when sales exploded, there was no hope of keeping up--and one of the most serious manufacturing problems was the bottleneck of collating the cards. By the February, 1984 Toy Fair, most of the major manufacturers offered triva games, which was projected to be the hottest category for the year.

R&R sold 580,000 units of the TV Guide game in 1984 at the full wholesale price of $12.50. There were few reorders after mid-October, as the market became saturated with trivia games (over 80 varieties) and "Trivial Pursuit" flooded the market. By Christmas 1984, all trivia games became heavily discounted; many retailers ran sales on "Trivial Pursuit" at $14.95, having paid $19.00.

Bad debts for Trivia Inc. were about $30,000 on approximately $7,000,000 billings, with hope of recovering $15,000. Losses from final inventory disposal (it was decided to close-out the game) were less than $100,000.

TV Guide was extremely pleased with the royalty collected from the venture. Kaplan, through his 50% ownership in Trivia Inc., made over $1,000,000 net. The total cost of designing and launching the product had been $50,000.

Commenting on the whole deal, Reiss said:

I think the critical aspects of success in being a contract manufacturer are to take care of your suppliers and to take care of your sales representatives. We want our suppliers to charge us full mark-up, so that we are a good customer to them, and we try hard to give them enough lead time to deliver. We pay on time always, no matter what happens. In exchange, we demand perfect work from them. They understand and like this relationship. We need their cooperation, because we are completely dependent on them.

The other aspect is how to deal with your customers, which for us are the manufacturer's representatives and the buyers of major chains. The manufacturer's reps are used to the fact that, when sales really do pick up in any product and they can make a lot of money, many manufacturers try to "shave" their commissions, perhaps feeling that they are making too much money. I never do that: I am happy if they make millions, and they know it. I also pay on time always. With this, I have developed a loyal and experienced work force and have no fixed or up-front sales cost.

All of these factors allowed us to move quickly. My contacts enabled me to print and manufacture the game for the same cost as a big company. But, a Parker Bros. or Milton Bradley would have incurred fixed costs of roughly $250,000 just for design and development and would then have committed to an advertising and promotion budget of at least $1 million.

The Future

According to Reiss, the big question at the end of 1984 was, "Do we add on a new version of the _TV Guide_ game, do a new trivia game, or go onto something new in spite of the great market penetration and success of our game?"

He had been doing some planning for a new game to be called "WHOOZIT?" and, instead of questions, it would show photographs of famous people that the players would have to recognize. He had a preliminary royalty deal with Bettman Archives, who had the exclusive marketing rights to all the photographs of the news service UPI, in addition to their own extensive archives. But, he was unsure about what the best follow-up for the success of 1984 could be.

The market, however, did not seem to be in the best condition. The 1984 Christmas season had ended with large unsold inventories of "Trivial Pursuit" and other trivia games. Some major companies, like Parker Bros., Lakeside, and Ideal, had closed out their games at low prices, further flooding the market. Many buyers were saying that trivia games, as a category, were over, although they seemed to accept Selchow's estimate of 7,000,000 units of "Trivial Pursuit" sold in 1985. That figure was well below the 20,000,000 units sold in 1984 but was still an exceptionally high figure compared with other board games. Selchow had also announced a plan to spend $5,000,000 to promote the game in 1985. Some upscale retailers, however, had announced their intention to abandon "Trivial Pursuit" and other trivia games, mostly because of the heavy discounting.

Reiss thought that one of the reasons why the public seemed to have lost interest in trivia games is that they were hard to play; too often, none of the players knew the answers. In retrospect, he thought that the TV Guide game had had the same problem. But, that would be different with "WHOOZIT?." He was thinking of making easier questions and giving several chances to each player and really expected the new game to be enjoyable.

In addition to improving the intrinsic playability of the game, Reiss wanted to have more flexibility selling it. He planned to offer three different price points; one of the versions having only the questions so it could be played on the "Trivial Pursuit" board. In spite of all these improvements, however, he was not sure whether he should try to replicate the success obtained with the TV Guide game and wondered what his best strategy for a follow-up could be.

Exhibit 1: Box of the Game

STYLE NO. 048

OVER 6000 TV TRIVIA QUESTIONS

- Drama • Sports • Comedy • News
- Soaps • Kid's • Specials • Movies
- Talk Shows • Quiz Shows and More!

Nothing mirrors our life and times like the electronic eye of television. For over 30 years, TV GUIDE has been writing the book on television every week. The TV GAME is both a nostalgic trip through the days of Lucy and Uncle Miltie, and an exciting journey through today's video environment...its people, its programs, and the world we all experience.

TRIVIA
INCORPORATED
230 Fifth Avenue, Suite 1104
New York, NY 10001 1 212-686-6003

Exhibit 2: Book with the questions

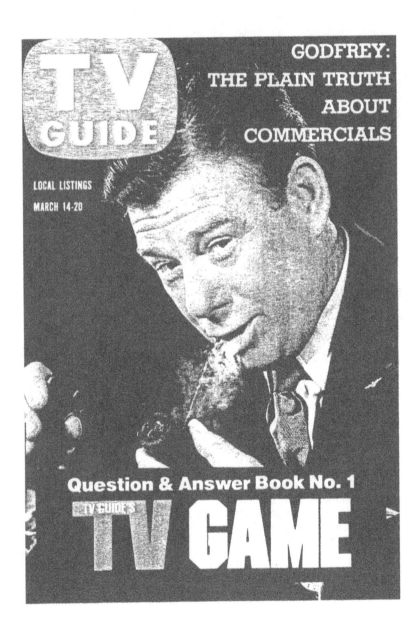

Exhibit 3: Stores to be reached

Sears	879
Penney	450.
Federated	451
Dayton Hudson	1149
R.H Macy	96
Allied Stores	596
Carter Hawley Hale	268
Associated Dry Goods	332
Mercantile	79
K mart	2174
Woolworth	N/A
Wal-Mart	751
T.G.&Y.	754
Zayre	848
Bradlees	132
Murphy	386
Rose's	195
Kay Bee	500
Spencer Gifts	450
Hook's Drug	120
Toys'R'Us	200

Bob Reiss thought that some 5,000 independent stores would be suitable targets, too.

Exhibit 4: Data on TV Guide's audience

February 3, 1984

Mr. Robert Reiss
President
R & R
230 Fifth Avenue
New York, New York 10001

Dear Bob:

I had our Research Department pull together some statistics about TV Guide that should be useful in discussing the audience dimensions of our magazine with major department stores and mass merchandisers.

First off, TV Guide's circulation averages over 17,000,000 copies each week.

Included in TV Guide's average issues audience are:
1. 37,838,000 adult readers age 18 and over.
2.   8,829,000 teenage readers 12-17.
3. 46,667,000 total readers age 12 and over.
4. 19,273,000 readers age 18-34.
5. 28,085,000 readers 18-49.
6. 10,312,000 adult readers in homes with one or more children 10-17 years of age.
7. 16,334,000 adult readers in homes with $25,000+ household income.
8. 11,815,000 adult readers with one or more years of college.
9.   4,344,000 adult readers who bought games or toys for children 12-17 in the past year.
10.   3,688,000 adult readers who bought games or toys for adults 18+ in the past year.

Exhibit 5: Letter to Supermarket buyers

TRIVIA
INCORPORATED
Exclusive Marketing Agent
R & R
230 Fifth Avenue, New York, NY 10001
1-212-686-6003 Telex 23R131-RR-UR

Mr. Lamar Williams   June 29, 1984
General Mdse. Buyer
JITNEY JUNGLE STORES of AMERICA
P.O. Box 3409
453 N. Mill St.
Jackson, MI 39207

Dear Mr. Williams:

Once every decade a product comes along that is just right!

We think we have that product for you. It has two key elements:

1.   It is licensed by TV GUIDE. I'm sure we don't have to tell you about the sales
       strength of TV GUIDE with its 17,000,000+ weekly circulation, 46,000,000 readers,
       etc. If your supermarket is typical, TV GUIDE is one of your best sellers and has
       earned its exalted position next to the cash registers.

2.   The Trivia Game explosion has taken America by storm and duplicated its Canadian
       heritage, where Trivia games have reigned for four years.

We have put these two elements together and with TV Guide's help, developed a new TV
GUIDE Trivia Game with over 6,000 questions and answers. The enclosed catalog sheet gives
full description and pricing. All our sales are final. We will advertise the game in 5 full color ads
in TV GUIDE this fall and will reach your customers.

We feel this game is ideally suited to be sold in your stores.
We would be happy to send you a sample and/or answer any questions you may have.

We look forward to the opportunity of working with you.

Sincerely,

Robert S. Reiss
Encl.

Exhibit 6: Ads in TV Guide magazine

Exhibit 7: Press releases on the game

The Indianapolis Star
INDIANAPOLIS, IND.
D. 225,148 SUN. 370.356

BURRELLE'S

The trivia edge

Walter Cronkite, reportedly a trivia game enthusiast, will have an edge if he plays *TV Guide's TV Game*, due in stores in June. The former *CBS Evening News* anchorman figures in more than a dozen of the 6,000 plus TV trivia questions in the new game.

MAY 26 1984

DAILY ⊙ NEWS
NEW YORK'S PICTURE NEWSPAPER®

4 STAR FINAL

★★★★ 30¢ | Tuesday, June 12, 1984 | Mostly sunny. Less humid. 85–90. Details p. 2

TV, too, gets into the trivia act

By BRUCE CHADWICK

SO YOU KNOW who was the only vice president to resign. So what? Okay, you know who threw the ball that Babe Ruth hit into the seats for his 60th home run. Big deal. And you know the name of the drummer in Glen Miller's band. Who cares?

Think you're so smart at trivia? All right, in addition to Matt Dillon, who was the only other character seen during the entire run of "Gunsmoke"? What business did John Walton and his father run in "The Waltons"? In the early days of "All in the Family," what was the name of the company where Archie Bunker worked?

Gotcha, didn't we? Well, to find out all the answers, see below, and also see "TV Guide's TV Game," the latest in the avalanche of trivia games that are flooding stores.

What's different about this one, though, is that it is limited to television.

It's a board game with cards and dice. You land on squares that have questions in seven categories: drama, sports, comedy, news, kids, movies and other TV (questions are divided into three levels of difficulty and many are aimed at today's youngsters and yes, there is a Mr. T question). Whoever gets the most right answers wins. The game is designed for individual or team play.

"Trivia games are hot because peo-

Milburn Stone

Mary Tyler Moore

ple are tired of video games and computer games in which the player is isolated," said Bob Reese, head of Trivia Inc. and the game's founder. "People want to play games with other people and match wits with talking faces, not TV screens. That, plus the yen for nostalgia, is making all trivia games, not just ours, big sellers."

Reese wanted to get into trivia games when Trivial Pursuit became a best seller last fall. He needed something different and turned to television.

"Everyone watches television, so

everyone will be interested in playing and, in fact, everyone will do reasonably well at this game," he said.

Reese turned to TV Guide because the magazine specializes in television coverage and has an extensive research department and library.

Researchers at TV Guide, led by Teresa Hagen, compiled a list of over 6,000 questions from over 20,000 submitted by writers there. Each question/answer had to have two written sources. Those that did not were dropped.

"It was harder than you'd think,"

said Hagen. "We needed a good balance of questions, easy to very difficult, and wanted a game that everyone, regardless of age, had a decent chance of winning."

The real research problems came in early television history.

"We had a very difficult time finding out firsts—the first comedy show, soap opera, president on TV, baseball game on TV—because early records were destroyed or sketchy."

They uncovered some unusual facts about television. As an example, the "Armed Forces Hour," an early '50s musical variety show, was only a half hour long. Dr. Ed Diethrich, owner of the USFL Arizona Wranglers, once performed open-heart surgery on live TV. Mary Tyler Moore's first major TV show was not "The Dick Van Dyke Show," but "Richard Diamond, Private Detective."

Hagen thinks the game is more than trivia. "We found that in playing it, we'd slide into conversations about what our own lives were like in relation to TV, like who our own heroes were, and our attitudes about things 20 years ago," she said. "We hope the game triggers conversations about life as well as TV."

The other continuing character on "Gunsmoke" was Doc Adams, played by Milburn Stone; the Waltons ran a lumber mill and Archie Bunker worked at Prendergast Tool and Die Co.

Appendix 1.
Bootstrap Tips Used in R & R Case Study

1. **VARIABLE COSTS**

   SALES REPS were paid on a commission basis only.

   ROYALTIES were paid to *TV Guide* were on a percentage basis. The percentage increased at certain volume levels. There were no upfront costs or guarantees.

   FACTOR was paid 1% of wholesale price or $.125 per game invoiced. The factor checked credit, collected monies for R&R, guaranteed all invoices, and performed some record keeping. R&R did not use them for advanced money against receivables, which was one of the reasons for a low fee. There was no guarantee of fees.

   INVENTOR was paid royalty on a percentage basis of invoiced games. He received no upfront or guaranteed payments.

   FULFILLMENT was done by Swiss Colony, which assembled all components of the game, stored them, and shipped them. They also billed our customers for every shipment, using our invoice. All these services were done for a cost to us of $.25 per game shipped.

2. **OUTSOURCING** was accomplished by ordering all components of game and having them shipped to Swiss Colony, who assembled, warehoused, and shipped. Trivia Inc. neither owned nor rented any facilities.

3. **SUPPLIERS** were responsible for our positive cash flow, quality, and on-time deliveries of components to Swiss Colony. This was primarily due to Sam Kaplan's strong credit and integrity rating. Our payment terms were 60-90 days while our selling terms were net 30 days.

4. **FACTORS** were used as described in the Variable Cost section.

5. **PUBLIC RELATIONS** were a strong asset. Howard Greene had a small entrepreneurial Public Relations company and handled the PR function for *TV Guide*. *TV Guide* management suggested we employ him to promote the game and that Trivia Inc. and *TV Guide* share the cost. We jumped at this very fair offer, and it turned out to be a wonderful decision. We received strong publicity for the game at a modest cost, and I made a lifelong friend.

6. **BARTER** was actually used in this venture although it was not in our original plans. After our contract was signed, I asked *TV Guide* for free ads in their large circulation, weekly publication. (I assumed they did not sell out the advertising every week.) Remember, there is no harm in asking. If you do, you'd be surprised how often your wish is granted. TV Guide came back to me and suggested they give me 5 pre-determined full-page color ads at no charge for increased royalty rates that would begin at established game volumes achieved. Each ad was worth $85,000. So basically we traded free ads for increased royalties, a Variable cost. That is Barter.

7. **FREE ADVERTISING** was used as described above. Actually it wasn't totally free as we had to give higher incremental royalty rates. However, no cash was involved, and the higher royalty rate meant nothing unless we achieved pretty high volume

levels.

8. **TESTING** was seriously employed. After the contract was signed, we created a high quality prototype of the game to bring to Toy Fair. The cost to produce this prototype was around $1,000. Utilizing this prototype and advancing our Ad program, we secured about $2,000,000 in advance orders. If the market had been negative to our plan and prototype, we would probably have aborted the project before we incurred the cost of developing 6,000 questions, artwork, and inventory.

9. **PRICING A PRODUCT** was an important part of our strategy. We knew going in that this was a short-term venture, a year at most. It doesn't make sense to pursue a venture with such a short life unless your margins are very good. We knew that Trivial Pursuit, which was driving this market, had a wholesale price of $19.00. We had a low cost on our game because of Sam Kaplan's idea of printing our 6,000 questions in 4 books, rather than on individual cards like Trivial Pursuit did. His approach gave us a product cost plus warehousing and shipping of $3.10 each. This allowed us to sell at $12.50 wholesale, which was a more than average margin. This while being substantially under Trivia Pursuit's $19.00.

 We knew the market could bear a high selling price (relative to cost) because Trivia games were a hot classification and our major competitor, Trivial Pursuit, was selling at a much higher price and was hopelessly back ordered.

10. **RELATIONSHIP BUILDING** was probably the number one Bootstrapping tip utilized. It permeated every aspect of the venture. Here are some of them:

Reiss-Kaplan: Kaplan owned the advertising agency Reiss used, and they knew each other for over 20 years and trusted each other. Kaplan was putting his money and time on the line, expecting that Reiss would put all the pieces together and successfully execute the plan. Reiss, on the other hand, trusted Kaplan to handle all the monies, develop the games' art, monitor Swiss Colony, and handle administrative details. For this, Reiss gave Kaplan 50% of the profits of Trivia Inc.

Reiss-Sales Reps: Reiss had over 25 years in the industry, developing relationships with the best Sales Reps. He gave the Reps exclusive rights to sell the games in their territories or selected accounts and paid above average commissions. The Reps trusted Reiss to pay full commissions on time and not drop them, cut commission rates, or reduce their territory—all problems Reps face when they sell hot items.

Reiss-Buyers: A high trust factor was developed between the parties over the years. This allowed Trivia Inc. to get $2,000,000 in advance orders without buyers seeing a finished product ... not the norm.

Kaplan-Swiss Colony: Kaplan not only handled their advertising, he was a paid consultant. This allowed him to get a lower Variable Cost deal and top-flight execution.

Kaplan-Suppliers: At the time, there was a shortage of paper in the country. Due to Kaplan's relationship with paper suppliers and printers, we received favorable credit terms and on-time deliveries.

Reiss-Inventor: Reiss had prior dealings with Alan Charles, who was a professional game designer. Charles traditionally worked on a guaranteed fee basis. In this case, he agreed to royalty only as he trusted he would be dealt with honestly. He also saw there was an opportunity to make more than his standard fee. He was right. When the venture ended, he received more than 18 times his regular fee.

Reiss-TV Guide: Although there was no prior relationship, a lot of trust was involved. Reiss trusted that after he told TV Guide his idea, they would not contact a large company like Parker

Bros. or Mattel and ask them to do it. There was no law to forbid their doing so. They asked Reiss for references. They were supplied with 13 references, which they checked at once. After checking, they immediately called Reiss to say they would go forward with the deal. So, there was a lot of trust/integrity with Reiss and the 13 people.

It should be apparent to you from all the space I have given to this point that I regard building trust from Day One as a cornerstone to a successful business and life.

11. **SELLING:** One of the major reasons that Reiss gave up 50% of Trivia Inc. was to free himself to devote most of his waking hours to selling. He solely sold some major accounts in the country like Sears, J.C. Penney, and Wal-Mart, made sales calls with his Reps on their major accounts, and monitored and motivated the Reps. The short window on this venture called for an all-out selling assault.

Appendix 2.
Tips for Getting an Appointment to Sell Something

It is important to have a good state of mind when attempting to get appointments with busy, important people. First, do not take rejection (non-answering of your calls and correspondence) personally. Your target may literally get 50 plus requests a day for an appointment. This is in addition to their regular extreme workload. Your challenge is to cut through this clutter. Stay upbeat. Never get angry. Follow up, be persistent, be creative. Be patient. Be confident. Be energetic. Smile. (Yes, you can sense a smile on the phone or through the written word.) Don't let Fear of Failure stop you from pursuing these hard to get appointments. A failure to secure the appointment can be a learning experience for your next attempt. Keep in mind the person you are trying to get an appointment with needs, wants, and even craves new ideas and innovative products and opportunities. You just have to get their attention for the opportunity to demonstrate you are the one to satisfy one of their needs.

The following are a random list of specific tips that may be helpful to you.

1. Write a short, concise, not longer than one page letter. The shorter, the better. Describe yourself or your company and why you are credible. State how the recipient of your letter will benefit from meeting with you. Don't exaggerate. Don't assume you'll never get a reply.
2. Send follow-up letter if no response. Think of sending via mail, fax, and email.
3. Email is the primary communications tool for many people. An advantage it offers is that the recipient usually reads it

himself/herself and, thus, the gatekeeper is bypassed. When sending email, give thought to your subject line. It will be short and needs to grab the reader's attention. State a benefit for the reader from meeting you, your service or product. A good subject line can prevent a delete.

4. Networking can be the most effective way to get an appointment with that busy, important person. Find a friend or business acquaintance of your target who you know and who will vouch for you. You almost certainly will get the target to take your call (which is a major part of the battle.) Always keep your network referrer abreast of the outcome of their introduction. Always send them a thank you note or call.

5. When you don't know who to contact in a company you want to do business with, writing to the president can be effective. Often, they will push the letter down to the proper person or immediate subordinates for handling. This person will often give you an appointment or contact you. They always follow up on their president's request as they are not sure if you are friendly with him/her. Sometimes the president will send you back your letter with a handwritten note on it to contact so and so in their company. You can then call that person and say the president of the company suggested you call them. They will take your call.

6. Phone for appointment. Many times you will have to get by the secretary or assistant. Try to start building a relationship with these gatekeepers. They may have more influence than you think. Try to find out a target's cell phone number.

7. Do your homework before attempting to get an appointment. Knowledge is power. Learn about the company (annual report, Internet, other vendors, trade magazines, etc.) the individual, the industry. This knowledge can help shape your approach, presentation, and ideas. It will also impress your target. People want to do business with smart people and with those who are prepared.

8. In your initial phone conversation for appointment, state concisely who you are and the purpose of the call. Try to listen carefully. You want to pick up problems the target has. Be ready with some key questions to get them talking. Solving problems gets you appointments and sales.

9. When you get your target on the phone, says Howard Hansen, a top insurance salesman, a good opening line might be: "Am I calling you at a bad time?" If person says, yes, he/she will suggest a better time. They will be more receptive to you then, appreciate your consideration, and the gatekeeper will more likely put the second call through, as you will say, "Mr. ____ asked me to call him today." If your target says no, this is a good time to talk, they will be more receptive to you as they will appreciate your concern for their needs, and they will invite you to continue. Remember, trying to persuade somebody when they are occupied with something else is stacking the deck against yourself.

10. For those people who have their calls screened, try calling before and after regular work hours when your target is more likely to answer.

11. If you are always sent to voice mail and get no replies, then think of leaving long but polite messages. Do this every day. Person may get annoyed, but will eventually tire of hearing your message to the end to be able to clear, and /or start to admire your persistence and call back.

12. Use humor as much as possible. Bookstores sell cartoon faxes for common circumstances . . . like someone not returning a phone call or answering a letter. Get a newspaper headline made up with target's name. Send letter or note in a unique package. (A package in a package in a package in a package, etc.) Send a chart with boxes to indicate reason your letters or calls are not answered. They should be a mix of funny and serious (never nasty). Include a stamped self-addressed letter. You do not need to be a joke teller to exhibit humor.

13. In attempting to cultivate a positive relationship with secretaries (gatekeepers) think of sending or giving them inexpensive humorous gifts like a head of lettuce, radishes, chocolate covered nuts, Jeeves, with a funny note. Corn often works.

14. Hire a sales rep, if appropriate, to set up the appointment. This applies to reps that know and do business with the buyer. (This is for cases where a buyer is the person with whom you want appointment.) For more information on how reps operate, see selling chapter.

15. Hand written faxes can be effective with certain people as they feel comfortable scribbling a quick answer rather than writing or dictating a letter.

16. Show up without an appointment, stating you were in the building. You will at least come person to person with the secretary or receptionist.

17. When leaving a phone message, give your phone number for a return call and say if you don't receive a return call, you will call next Tuesday at 2:00 p.m. This lets the recipient know you will call back. Hopefully, they will tell their secretary to take the call and put it through.

18. If you sell a product that could possibly be sold in a gift store, make a deal to have a display of it in the gift store of the hotel where your targeted person stays during conventions, trade shows, etc. To do so, you can guarantee the sale to store or offer it free of charge. You, of course, would have to research dates your person will be there.

19. If you do get through on the phone and your person says he just does not have time to see you as he or she will be traveling the next two months, then ask to have an appointment with them in one of the cities they will be visiting. Or offer to meet them at the airport and fly on the same plane or offer to drive them to the airport. They should be impressed by your determination and creativity.

20. If person you want to see has set buying hours to see new vendors, make your call on a horrible weather day. This will mean there will be few people that day and possibly impress your person with your fortitude in coming to see him/her in such terrible weather.

21. If your prospect lives in another city, call and say you plan to be in their city in two weeks for say two days, and you would appreciate an appointment during your stay there.

22. Old-fashioned politeness can go a long way in achieving your objectives. Follow up thank you notes and a simple use of the words, "Please" and "Thank you" are effective.

23. If you finally win your hard-earned appointment and your target cancels (and sometimes doesn't even let you know), don't get angry. Look at it as an opportunity. Immediately and cheerfully set up a new appointment. In most cases your target is aware of the inconvenience they caused you and will be more receptive and prone to give you a chance by buying into your idea or product. The cause of the cancellation could be an emergency, their boss calling them, or even forgetfulness in a hectic schedule. If cancellations reoccur and target doesn't apologize, then you have a good reason to go over their head to their superior.

24. Try some out of the box approaches to get noticed. Think about stretching your comfort zone. Some examples:

   a. Buy an inexpensive watch (Wal-Mart around $6.00) Cover 15 minutes of the face with a label and send watch without box to your target, asking for 15 minutes of their time. Recipient will usually take notice. They face a dilemma. They don't know the cost of the watch. They probably can't keep it. It's a pain to return it. Maybe, they will be intrigued by your creativity and give you your appointment.

b. Send your target a live lottery ticket with a note that their odds of receiving value are greater hiring or seeing you than winning with this lottery ticket. However, you wish them well with the ticket. Human nature says he won't throw away a chance to win the lottery. As he or she follows the ticket, they will think of you ... What's to lose? There should be no embarrassment trying these and other innovative but offbeat approaches. Brainstorm other oddball approaches.

25. When you do get your appointment, immediately send a short follow up note or email confirming it. (Sometimes executives who make appointments forget to tell their secretary who then may schedule another one for the same time slot.)

26. A good line when calling for an appointment is to ask your prospect for 6 minutes of their time. The request and oddball number is intriguing and takes little of their time. Rik Talley, the VP of Sales for Logo, has been using this for years with great success.

27. Be persistent. Keep following up until you succeed. Many people test for persistency.

Appendix 3.
Cash Flow Statement

Projecting cash flow is one of the most important ways you can use numbers to manage and grow your business. The cash flow statement also can have important outside-world significance, since you'll probably have to submit a cash flow statement in almost all cases where you're looking for outside money.

Let me try to walk you though a typical cash flow exercise. I'll begin by summarizing the six steps you'll have to take before generating the cash flow statement. Then I'll go back and explain each of these six in depth:

This explanation is based on a physical product business. If you are a service business, everything remains the same except you need not be concerned with inventory, components, or returns.

1. List all the assumptions you will make in creating this statement.
2. Project monthly sales for the entire year.
3. Add up all cash revenues for each month.
4. Add up all cash expenditures for each month.
5. Subtract your expenditures (#4) from your revenues (#3) to determine your monthly balance, which can be a plus or a minus.
6. Do a monthly cumulative cash position (in other words, a summary of your #5's). This can be a positive or a negative number. This is the critical step in determining when in the year you will need more cash (the minuses), and when you will have the cash needed to pay back loans or pay bonuses (the pluses).

1. ASSUMPTIONS

Before laying out your numbers, you should list the assumptions that you will use in determining some of those numbers. Here is a sample list of some general ones you'll need to make. Your specific type of business will probably require others.

- Determine your average receivables. (How many days will it take for you to receive your check after the invoice is made and the receivable is created?) You might also build in the number of days it takes for the bank to clear your deposited checks.
- What is your average rate of commission and what percentage of sales are commissionable? In this vein, when do you pay these commissions—e.g., 15 days after the close of the month for the previous month's shipments? Or—as at some companies—do you pay commissions when the bill is paid?
- What is your average cost of goods, which will determine your average gross margin? For instance: every $1000 of sales will yield you $450 of profit. Therefore, your average cost of goods is 55% (550 divided by 1,000). You will need this percentage when determining your cash outlay for purchases, which will vary by your sales projections.
- How far in advance must you purchase products or components before you ship goods and pay these vendors? Must you pay vendors upon receipt, or—if not—how many days afterward? If your product is made overseas, do you pay before receipt, and if so, how much before?
- Do the different components of your cost-of-goods-sold have different cash requirements? That is usually true in a manufacturing business. Purchases, for example, may have a 30-day turnaround, where labor may need to be paid every week.
- If any of your products need to have royalties paid, when are those royalties due? Monthly? Quarterly? How soon after the close of the period?

- If you have a debt, how much interest is paid, and when is it paid?
- When is the principal due?
- When are taxes due, and when are they paid?
- When are insurance payments due?
- What new hires will you make, and when? What wage increases will be given (if any)?
- How much inventory will you need to maintain in anticipation of orders, and what rate of turn do you anticipate on it?
- If you give cash discounts, how many dollars of receivables will be affected by those discounts, and how much sooner will the receivable become cash?
- How many of your vendors offer cash discounts for early payment, and how many dollars of your payables will be affected, and for how much in terms of dollar savings?

2. PROJECTING MONTHLY SALES

To do this, you can look at last year's sales (assuming this is at least your second year in business) as a guide. As you record each month's sales, indicate any large orders you received. When you look at the figures next year, you can think about whether that large order is likely to be repeated. Be sure to recognize the seasonal nature of your business—if any—in your projections. Don't just do averages!

Remember that last year's numbers are history, and that projections are looking into the future. The more mature your business is, the more likely that the past has a correlation to the future. Newer companies or those with fad products should rely less on the past to project the future.

Your sales management and sale force should give key inputs into developing sales projections. The entrepreneur/manager needs to know the sales people well in order to figure out whether they are giving him or her inflated sales projections (to ensure adequate inventory to maximize sales and commissions). Large customers should also be consulted in this forecasting. The good ones should cooperate with you on this as it is in their best interest to do so. They want you to have enough inventory to maximize their sales as well. Again, someone in your company needs to know the buyer in question to determine his or her reliability in putting forth purchase expectations.

One thing is for sure: your accountant, bookkeeper, or chief financial officer should not be the only person involved in creating your sales projections. Triangulate—use one person's information to verify or contradict another's.

Another element of this monthly projection is a number for average returns, whether due to quality problems or plain old customer dissatisfaction. If this number historically runs at 5 percent, then this figure should be deducted from your projected sales figure. If you don't, your planned revenues are likely to experience a mysterious 5 percent shortfall.

3.   MONTHLY CASH RECEIPTS

These revenues will consist of the following components:

- Collection of receivables
- Cash sales (if any)
- Royalty, commission, or fees income
- Sale of assets
- Miscellaneous income (such as rebates)
- Loans or sale of stock

4.   MONTHLY CASH EXPENDITURES

I like to divide my cash costs into *fixed* and *variable*. The fixed costs are usually the same every month, regardless of volume. The variable costs can change with volume (or cost in a certain percentage). Some fixed costs (e.g., rent) are paid every month, and others (e.g., insurance, taxes) fall only in certain months.

Examples of fixed costs:

- Rent
- Wages and payroll taxes
- Telephone
- Office supplies
- Utilities
- Postage
- Travel and entertainment
- Leases (computes, faxes, cars, etc.)
- Accounting/legal
- Insurance
- Interest expense
- Subscriptions

Examples of variable costs:

- Commissions
- Royalties (can sometimes be fixed, or a combination of fixed and variable)
- Warehouse expenses
- Advertising (can also be fixed)
- Purchases (can also be fixed)

Some expenses can be a combination of fixed and variable, such as a warehouse expense that is based on a percentage of dollar shipments but has a guaranteed monthly minimum. Insurance of goods shipped can be variable, while health insurance is fixed only if the number of employees remains constant. Liability insurance can be either fixed or variable.

There are also onetime expenses that draw on your cash, such as equipment purchases or project-based consulting fees.

Whatever cash payments are made during the year should be accounted for in this cash flow statement under "monthly cash expenditures." Some expenditures, like the phone bill, are fixed (in that they occur every month), but can vary. In these cases, take your best guess, which can be based on last year's bills, or on your estimate of increased or decreased activity in certain months. And don't forget to add a "Miscellaneous" expense line because you can be sure that here will be expenses you haven't thought of.

5. DETERMINE THE MONTHLY BALANCE.

This is the bottom line for each month: whether you plan to take in more receipts than expenditures going out, or vice versa. It is a simple calculation: subtract the sum of all your monthly expenditures (#4) from the sum of all your receipts (#3).

6. MONTHLY CUMULATIVE CASH POSITION

This is simply a running total of all your pluses and minuses each month (5), added to or subtracted from the cash on hand you started with each month.

For example: let's say you started January 1 with a cash balance of $135,000. For the month of January, you spend $60,000 and have receipts of $52,000. Therefore, you have a negative monthly balance of $8,000. This is subtracted from the opening cash balance of $135,000, leaving you with an end-of-month cash balance of $127,000. This $127,000 then becomes the opening cash balance for February.

These ending cumulative figures are critical in determining future cash needs or when you can pay back existing loans. As soon as they become negative, then you know that in that month, you will need additional funds to cover that negative figure. You may conclude that you'll have a negative cumulative figure in only three months a year.

With that knowledge, you can go to your bank for a short-term loan and show them your cash flow statement which will indicate the month you will have enough of a surplus of cash to repay the loan.

Build in a mid-month cash cushion or at least be very aware of the need for it. Your receipts may come in at the end of the month, and in the meantime you may incur expenses (such as payroll or contract labor) that can't wait until the end of the month.

In another scenario, a monthly cumulative negative number may persuade you to go see some key suppliers to get an additional amount of time to pay your bills. An extension from 30 days to 60 days on your payable terms can have a big positive impact on your cash flow statement.

This cash flow statement is a document that needs to be revised regularly. If you are flush with cash, you might only want to revise it quarterly. If you're in a tight position, however, you'll need to revisit it monthly (or even more often). A change in sales from your forecast can dramatically alter your needs. A sudden large increase in sales is not necessarily good news, as it will require more cash to support it than you have budgeted for that purpose. (Of course, I'd rather have that problem than a sales shortfall!)

The message is: *Pay extremely close attention to this statement or you can find yourself in serious trouble!*

Once again, I strongly recommend that you take the time to get comfortable with all this stuff. Why? Because cash is the lifeblood of your company. Businesses fail for lots of reasons ranging from bad ideas to bad execution. But the immediate reason for most failures— the "proximate cause" as the lawyers put it—is running out of cash. Yes, many entrepreneurs run a good show without any formal cash flow statements. I've never met a good one yet who didn't have all the critical information (cash positions, cash needs) in their heads. The ones who worried least about cash flow, at least temporarily, were those who were flush with cash.

Most of us aren't so lucky. The best way to inoculate yourself against running out of cash is to have solid knowledge in advance about your cash needs. Your accountant or financial adviser may have ideas about how to generate numbers that represent your particular business most effectively. (There are computer programs on the market that help you generate cash flow statements in a generic kind of way, but these may not give proper weight to the most important variables of your particular business.) However you generate your statement, it's absolutely imperative that you understand how this statement works and what all of its component parts are. I can't state this too forcefully. You can't make the daily decisions you need to make to run your company if you aren't' the master of your cash needs.

Your statement shows your peak cash needs and when they will occur. By understanding your impending cash peaks and valleys, you can start planning exactly how you're going to handle any cash crunches that hit the company. And planning is the key idea here. It takes time to borrow or otherwise raise money. You will be able to make better deals if you're not under a cash-crunch gun. And as noted above, if you're jumping off the equity cliff—selling stock to raise money—your investment bankers and venture capitalists will need clear proof that you have a firm handle on your business.

I probably don't have to tell you that the only constant in business is *change*. Sales forecasts—a key component in building the cash flow statement—change constantly. Each of these changes means changes (big or little) in your cash flow. Changes in product costs, seasonal costs, advertising costs, capital needs, and market opportunities all necessitate changes in your cash flow statement. Computers are extremely helpful here because you can change one or more assumptions and watch the impact of those changes flow through without having to do endless number-crunching. But once again: *You've got to be in charge of these exercises.* An assumption is only useful if you understand it and why you're tinkering with it. When the assumptions start getting built into the program and you stop understanding them, you're probably heading for trouble.

Appendix 3: Cash Flow Statement

To help you better understand this **Simplified Cash Flow Statement**, here is an example with real numbers for a 12 month statement. An analysis of the statement follows, highlighting problems and offering potential solutions.

ASSUMPTIONS

average receivables	30 days
selling terms	net: 30 days
* cost of goods sold	55%
* average sales commission	7% (including non-commission sales)
sales commission	payable month after sale
purchases	paid in 15 days
* royalties	6% (takes into account non-royalty sales; due month after sale)
* bad debts/returns	3%
* warehouse expense	6% payable month after shipping (net 30 days)
advertising/sales promotion	4% of projected yearly sales, spent in last 5 months of year
wages	$180,000/year ($60,000 for owner/ entrepreneur and balance for 4 employees last 5 months of year

* Variable Expense

Projected Monthly Sales

December (previous year)	$120,000[1]
January	60,000
February	45,000
March	40,000
April	40,000
May	35,000
June	35,000
July	30,000
August	50,000
September	80,000
October	120,000
November	250,000
December	135,000
PROJECTED YEAR	$920,000

[1]December Sales of $120,000-$3,600 (3% Bad Debts) = $116,00

	JAN	FEB	MAR	APR	MAY
Accounts receivable collections *116,400		58,200	43,650	38,800	38,800
Other income	-------	-------	-------	-------	-------
Total Cash Receipts	116,400	58,200	43,650	38,800	38,800
Cash paid out					
Purchases/materials	**64,020	32,010	24,750	22,000	22,000
Sales Commissions	8,400	4,200	3,150	2,800	2,800
Royalties	7.200	3,600	2,700	2,400	2,400
Warehouse	7,200	3,600	2,700	2,400	2,400
Advertising/Sales Promotion	-------	-------	-------	-------	-------
Rent	3.500	3.500	3.500	3.500	3.500
Wages/officer salaries	15,000	15,000	15,000	15,000	15,000
Leases	2,000	2,000	2,000	2,000	2,000
Accounting/ Legal	700	700	700	700	700
Telephone	400	400	400	400	400
Office Supplies	150	150	150	150	150
Interest	-------	-------	-------	-------	-------
Insurance	800	800	800	800	800
Travel & Entertainment	600	600	600	600	600
Purchases/fixed assets					
Miscellaneous	500	500	500	500	500
	-------	-------	-------	-------	-------
Total cash Paid Out	110,470	67,060	56,950	57,750	53,000
Monthly cash surplus (Deficit)	5,930	(8,860)	(13,300)	(18,950)	(14,200)
Beginning Cash Balance	27,000	32,930	24,070	10,770	(8,180)
End of Month Cash Balance	32,930	24,070	10,770	(8,180)	(22,380)

**55% (Cost of Goods) of $120,000 (Dec. Sales) =$66,000 –3% (Bad Debts/ Returns) $1,980 = $64,020

JNE	JULY	AUG	SEPT	OCT	NOV	DEC	JAN
3,950	33,950	29,100	48,500	77,600	116,400	242,500	130,950
				10,000	10,000	10,000	
3,950	33,950	29,100	48,500	87,600	126,400	252,500	130,950
9,250	19,250	16,500	27,500	44,000	66,000	137,500	74,250
2,450	2,450	2,100	3,500	5,600	8,400	17,500	9,450
2,100	2,100	1,800	3,000	4,800	7,200	15,000	8,100
2,100	2,100	1,800	3,000	4,800	7,200	5,000	8,100
-------	-------	7,360	7,360	7,360	7,360	7,360	------
3,500	3,500	3,500	3,500	3,500	3,500	3,500	3,500
5,000	15,000	15,000	15,000	15,000	15,000	15,000	15,000
2,000	2,000	2,000	2,000	2,000	2,000	2,000	2,000
700	700	700	700	700	700	700	700
400	400	400	400	400	400	400	400
150	150	150	150	150	150	150	150
800	800	800	800	800	800	800	800
600	600	600	600	600	600	600	600
500	500	500	500	500	500	500	500
-------	-------	-------	-------	-------	-------	-------	-------
9,550	49,550	53,210	68,010	90,210	119,810	216,010	123,550
5,600)	(15,600)	(24,110)	(19,500)	(2,610)	6,590	36,490	7,400
2,380)	(37,980)	(53,580)	(77,690)	(97,190)	(99,800)	(93,210)	(56,720)
7,980)	(53,580)	(77,690)	(97,190)	(99,800)	(93,210)	(56,720)	(49,320)

COMMENTS ABOUT THIS
CASH FLOW STATEMENT

The statement clearly indicates that this company needs more cash, and also when it needs that extra cash (in April with the peak need in October). Finally, it shows that the company will lose money for the year. What it doesn't show, and what you should understand, is that most of the time things don't go as well as projected, and your company is likely to need even more money than you predicted.

It's clear that some decisions have to be made at this company. One response would be to accept the loss for this year and hope things improve next year. (This assumes that the company's managers can get the cash needed to get through the year.) More proactively, the company's leaders could change assumptions, strategies, overheads, etc., to respond to the problem indicated by the projection.

Let's look at some specifics.

The yearly breakeven for this company, based on all costs in this statement, is $1,359,473. Here is how this figure was arrived at:

Variable Expenses	Percentage
Cost of goods sold	55%
Sales commission	7%
Royalties	6%
Warehouse	6%
Bad debts	3%
Advertising	4%
Total variable	81%
Contribution margin	19%

Fixed costs monthly = $23,650 (rent, $3,500; wages, $15,000; lease, $2,000; accounting/legal, $700; phone, $400; office supplies, $150; insurance, $800; T&E, $600; miscellaneous, $500)

Yearly fixed costs = $283,800 ($23,650 x 12)

However, there was $30,000 in other income for October, November, and December, and there was a onetime asset purchase in April for $4,500.

This leaves an additional net income of $25,500, which reduces the yearly fixed cost to $258,300.

The break-even figure is obtained by dividing the yearly fixed cost ($258,300) by the gross profit margin (19%), in this instance, of $1,359,473.

What else can we learn from looking at this example?

The company's largest negative ending cash balance of $99,800 is reached in October.

By January, the peak need is reduced by $50,000 to $49,320.

So the cash flow statement clearly tells the "numbers story" for the year.

How can that story be improved? Here are six possible approaches:

1. The company could meet its additional $100,000 peak need by borrowing it, or by securing additional capital. The company would be able to pay back $45,000 of the $100,000 by January, so perhaps a short-term loan of $50,000 and additional capital of $50,000 is the way to go. If the company borrows the money, of course, it will have to add the interest payments into the cash flow calculations. This will slightly alter the break-even and peak-needs calculations. (There is a line in the statement for these expenditures.)

2. Additional sales of $526,315 would mean that the company would not need the $100,000. Of course, the company would have to decide how realistic this extra sales figure would be to achieve, and whether this would require any additional fixed expense.

3. The company could increase its profit margin of 19% to reduce its additional cash needs. This could be done (for example) by lowering the cost of goods through better purchasing, or by cutting the variable costs. When cutting these costs, of course, the company has to decide whether such cuts might adversely affect sales projections.

   If the company increased its gross margin by 5%—that is, up to 24%—its breakeven would be reduced to $1,076,250, and it would need to raise $46,000 less ($920,000 x .05). You could also raise prices to increase profit margins, but usually this isn't feasible.

4. The company could cut back on fixed expenses. Maybe it could let one or two people go, using temps when absolutely necessary, and also nibble away at other cost items.

5. The company could use a combination of all of the above.

6. You might approach your suppliers to seek better payment terms, say net 60 instead of net 15. Now run the numbers with an additional 45 days to pay for your purchases and see how much it will reduce your cash peak needs. This is a perfect example of how a computer software program can quickly crunch the change in numbers.

   My point is that this cash flow statement clearly articulates a need to *act*. It tells the manager how much action is needed, and it suggests areas in which actions might be taken.

   Finally, remember that this is an ever-changing document. You will need to update it, and analyze it, constantly.

About the Author

BOB REISS GREW UP IN BROOKLYN and attended the New York City public schools. He is a graduate of Columbia University (where he played on an undefeated basketball team). He is a U.S. Army veteran, and a Harvard Business School graduate. He has been involved in 16 start-ups and is the founder of a number of highly successful companies, including Reiss Games, R&R, and Valdawn, Inc., a division of R&R. R&R/Valdawn was named to the Inc. 500 list of America's fastest-growing companies for three years in a row.

He has been the subject of two Harvard Business School cases— taught at more than 100 institutions around the world—and has been a guest speaker in entrepreneurship classes at the undergraduate, graduate, and executive levels both nationally and internationally.

His other book is *Low Risk High Reward*. He is married to an entrepreneur and has five daughters.

CPSIA information can be obtained
at www.ICGtesting.com
Printed in the USA
BVOW11s0940120118

504931BV00002B/224/P